MY JOB ISN'T WORKING!

10 PROVEN WAYS TO BOOST YOUR CAREER MOJO

MICHAEL BROWN

First published in Great Britain by Practical Inspiration Publishing, 2018

ISBN 978-1-788-600-22-4

Practical Inspiration
PUBLISHING

Praise for *My Job Isn't Working!*

This book could not be more timely. Too many employees are struggling to maintain a healthy mojo at work, and My Job Isn't Working! will help them to recover it. The tools are introduced in an accessible and highly pragmatic style, and it felt like a shot of adrenaline to read.

Marshall Goldsmith, Thinkers50 World's #1 Executive Coach, #6 Most Influential Business Thinker 2017 and author of *Mojo: How to Get It, How to Keep It and How to Get It Back if You Lose It*

Michael's aim of helping mid-career workers to deal with the unprecedented pressures of today's workplace is something which resonates fully with me. It is both timely and relevant – an admirable initiative.

Nancy Kline, founding director of Time To Think Ltd and best-selling author of the *Time To Think* book series

The generous gift of this book is to supply readers with the encouragement, insights and tools to work around dysfunctional workplaces by helping them to reboot their self-awareness, self-empowerment and self-confidence to engage

in more effective and satisfying behaviour – despite the many dysfunctions that may persist in their current situation.

Dr Ralph H. Kilmann, co-author of the Thomas-Kilmann Instrument (TKI) and CEO of KilmannDiagnostics.com

Too many people experience work as a turn-off or a trap. But it doesn't have to be that way. Here is a useful guide from an experienced voice that will help individuals in mid-career to change things for the better. It shows that small shifts can have a big impact.

Rob Goffee, Emeritus Professor of Organisational Behaviour at the London Business School and co-author of *Why Should Anyone Be Led by You?*

It can be tough working in the "squeezed middle" of a modern organization. We experience faster pace of change and increasing demands to deliver. At the same time, it can be hard to get things done in a day filled with unnecessary meetings, irrelevant communication and unclear processes. No wonder some people lose what Michael calls their "career mojo".

Low levels of engagement and enthusiasm are a problem for businesses and a tragedy for individuals – life is too short to not enjoy something you spend so much time on. Michael's book delves into why we can sometimes lose our career mojo and offers some practical suggestions on how you can regain it. Don't wait for someone else to do it for you.

Kevan Hall, CEO of Global Integration, author of the books *Speed Lead*, *Making the Matrix Work* and *Kill Bad Meetings*

In My Job Isn't Working!*, Michael has woven together insights and the experience of more than twenty years of coaching and training. He has created an immensely practical guide which offers the reader a host of realistic and actionable ways to*

rediscover fulfilment in the workplace. Particularly for those who might feel that they're at a crossroads, or simply need to re-inject greater enthusiasm into their daily working lives, My Job Isn't Working! *offers not only hope but the means to take positive action. What is perhaps most encouraging is that Michael has used these techniques himself, not only to identify his true vocation but to find the satisfaction that was previously missing in his career. It is an inspirational book that helps others to identify their dreams and then to pursue them in very tangible ways.*

Ian Walker, Operations Director in the tech sector

This book is excellent. It's very engaging and full of great tips, ideas and anecdotes: a really good read with outstanding tools and ideas.

Guy Arnold, business coach and author of *Sales Through Service* and *Slow Selling*

In My Job Isn't Working! *Michael addresses the barriers preventing employees from realising their full potential and their ability to achieve more for their organisation. I believe this book is of genuine value because the advice offered is so accessible and practical, and I have no hesitation in recommending it.*

Ray Bremner OBE, retired President and CEO,
Unilever Japan

This book is a timely reminder that companies succeed or fail on the performance of their mid-career managers, but often forget them when training, motivation and reward programmes are developed. It's time for their voice to be heard.

Peter Vicary-Smith, Chief Executive, Which?

I loved the book and want to order a copy when it's out for everyone on my team!

Petra Merne, Director, Global Marketing, OPP Limited

Having known and partnered closely with Mike over many years, it is great to see that this book has been written so true to his own voice. Mike's self-effacing tone and his lightness of touch help to make such a serious subject accessible. He has inspired me in the past, and I am sure this book will do the same for its readers.

Spencer Holmes, Chief Operations Officer, Totem Learning

Dedication

If, from about 4pm onwards on Sunday afternoons, you start to feel slightly nauseous and lose your appetite at the prospect of the arrival of Monday morning (we used to call it "Sundayitis" in my family): this book is dedicated to you.

If on Monday mornings your heart sinks when the alarm goes off because you realise it is in fact Monday morning: I dedicate this book to you, too.

If you find yourself wondering how on earth you got to be in this job and what you can do to bring it closer to what you had in mind when you first started it: this book is my gift to you.

If you find yourself avoiding your boss but wishing you could get to know each other better: this is for you.

To all employees, at whatever stage of your career, feeling the pressure and wondering how to respond to what is coming at you: I get it. I feel your pain, because I've been there.

Finally, to my parents, Jim and Janet, who stretched themselves financially to the limit (and sometimes beyond, I fear) to fund my schooling. A classical education at Eton gave me the gift of writing fluently, as well as confidence and self-belief. Oxford taught me how to think and organise myself. Dad, you were a black-belt proofreader who managed to find errors galore in the books you read (all underlined with a sharp pencil). I could have done with your skills. Mum, I'd have turned to you for some of your passion and energy when I got stuck. I think you'd both have enjoyed reading this, and it would have made you proud. Thank you.

This book is for all of you.

Contents

Foreword

A few years ago, I travelled to another planet. My company had been acquired by a large European multinational and some time after the transition I agreed to move to London to run a larger part of the parent organisation in Europe.

Moving from running a company in Silicon Valley to managing and leading a large team in an even larger European business was a shock, to say the least. As I began to get my bearings, I realised that I had landed on Mars.

In Silicon Valley, passion, purpose and mission are the foundation on which companies and careers are built. People change jobs frequently based on opportunity and the fortunes of the companies they are with. Fast trackers scramble up the career ladder, learning as quickly as their jobs will teach them.

For many of the people in my new team, scattered across Spain, the UK, Israel and the US, working for one of the world's largest companies was the basis for their entire career. They had joined soon after finishing university, learned the rules of the game, and worked diligently to further themselves within the set of opportunities and well-defined career ladder characteristic of a massive corporate environment. For many of them, simply having a stable and reliable job through the financial crisis of 2008–2009 and the drawn-out recession that followed throughout Europe was a huge win.

But after 10, 20 or even 30 years in the same place, while most of my team still cared deeply about the work they personally did, passion, purpose and mission were not top of mind when many of them thought about the path they were on. The challenge of helping these people shake things up presented the opportunity for a double win: helping individuals rekindle the fire that burned deep within them, and helping the company by re-energising a part of its workforce.

Too many executives think managing and leading is simply about delivering this quarter's results on the way to delivering this year's results. While financial results are what shareholders look for, people are what it takes to deliver them. Nothing happens without a motivated workforce, at least not for very long. Investing in your team, in their development, in their well-being – this is what a successful leader needs to do if they want to look after next year's results, and the results the year after that. Focusing on relationships, on people, on making sure that people are in the right jobs and can see a path forward for themselves – this is the secret to looking ahead on the road to success. These are the investments you can make in the short term that will yield sustained rewards. Corporate success is a marathon, not a sprint. And that holds true on a personal level, as well.

In my situation, arriving fresh into an established organisation, simply setting a vision and direction and communicating those throughout the team was not going to be sufficient. Necessary, yes, but we needed to move beyond that. We needed to help our people find their way forward, in the context of the plan that we were setting for the organisation.

Enter Michael Brown, who joined us to bring to life my aim of helping leaders and managers re-discover who they were, remember what they cared about, and learn a new set of tools to help them and their teams navigate the journey in front of them. Michael and I, supported by a stellar team that helped us develop and focus the content, barnstormed our way across the world, delivering and delivering (and delivering again!) a three-day interactive workshop that brought people face to face with new ideas about management and leadership, infused them with new energy, and asked them to look deep within themselves to remember what made them tick.

Across geographies, across cultures, with 25-year careerists and with people almost fresh out of school, the impact was tremendous. We witnessed individuals have transformative moments and teams break through years-old barriers. We inspired groups to confront unproductive behaviours; we watched as incredibly brave team members shared vulnerabilities with colleagues and asked for help and support. We asked every participant to commit to specific actions based on the insights they'd gathered, with focused application on their own strengths and weaknesses. For some people, the impact of the session came to life immediately – we could see it in their work and in their relationships. For others, the insights they developed ran so deep that they were still wrestling with the full magnitude of the implications months later.

Almost to a person, participants described it as the most impactful corporate training they'd ever been through. The reason was simple: we weren't training people on a company vision, or a product, or a process. Instead, we focused on equipping people with the tools they needed to better understand themselves, to better understand their teams and to better understand the environment around them. We asked them to think about what got them up in the morning, what they cared most about and how work could be more than just a job. We asked them what it would take for their jobs to be emotionally, intellectually and spiritually rewarding – not just a way to pay the bills. And we gave the same back to them – from the highest-level executive in my organisation down, we shared with them what made us tick.

Through the course of this training, we built relationships. Up and down, sideways, crossways. I used this opportunity to get to know them, and let them get to know me. The value of building relationships in a hugely complex organisation should never be underestimated. When you know the people you're trying to collaborate with, when you know how their minds work, what's important to them and what their goals are, you're oiling the entire machine. Everything from that point forward goes faster and more easily.

In a world that is moving increasingly quickly, facing business challenges that are becoming more and more dynamic, and with information that despite its growing volume is rarely definitive, there is no better investment than truly knowing yourself, your team and the company around you.

When I first read an early draft of this book, I realised immediately that Michael had taken that ethos and bottled it. He's brought together his experience from across many companies – not just the one I worked at – and his experience with people at all points in their careers and assembled a step-by-step guide that lets you facilitate the same kind of introspection and self-development that he and I spent weeks together delivering in the classroom.

The trick here, the same as it was with Michael at the front of the room, is that this isn't a passive experience. It just doesn't work that way. In the classroom we would tell people that if they just sat back and listened passively, they'd be wasting the next three days of their life. To get something out of it, they needed to engage.

The same is true with this book: you're only going to get out of it what you choose to put into it. Big gains will come only if you put in the effort, if you're prepared to undertake some deep reflection, and if you're willing to be brutally honest with yourself.

But if you're up for it, this book will help you. It can help you understand yourself better; it can help improve your current work environment; it can help you figure out if you need to make a change, and which way you should be looking next.

If you're ready for it, I see Michael at the front of the class and an empty seat right at the front. Time to step on in.

Ian Small

Former Chief Data Officer

Telefónica Group

Introduction

"I know well what I am fleeing from but not what I am in search of."

Michel de Montaigne

Wakey wakey!

I have spent the past 18 years in training rooms around the world working with people from all types of businesses. I must have met nearly 10,000 people in that time, normally for at least one day. This book is based on what people have told me during that time. In the safe and high-trust environment of a training room I've seen for myself what people who have lost their career mojo look and sound like. These are the sorts of things they say:

> *"There is no point sticking your head over the parapet because it will get blown off."*

> *"I have had five managers in three years and have yet to meet one face to face."*

> *"I work on Sundays to make Monday mornings less miserable."*

> *"We're too busy working down in the weeds to review anything and learn from experience. We're a bunch of busy fools."*

"We're not allowed to ask why: that's seen as being difficult."

These are symptoms of organisational dysfunctionality. As a result, the engine which drives people at work – their career mojo, I call it – has either broken down or needs a boost. What is perhaps even more worrying is that too many people do not recognise it.

They think this is normal.

Someone once summed it up beautifully for me: "We've fallen asleep at the wheel." They are drifting along like I did when I worked in corporate land, hoping something might turn up. It probably won't – in fact, for reasons I'll expand on later, I'd confidently predict that workplace dysfunctionality is going to get far more acute over the coming years.

What do people with career malfunction look like? Dispirited. Tired. Stressed. Emotional. Nervous. Cautious. Wary of opening up. Distracted. Defensive. They not only feel different, they look different.

What does that look like in a training room? People don't like putting their phones away. They walk into a room full of people who work in the same organisation and are there to learn with them, and (sometimes without saying a word) they jump onto their laptop. The room fills with people but remains silent. They are a little thrown by a handshake. They are not great at introducing themselves. They worry about finishing on time. They turn up without anything to write with (knowing that we are going to be spending three days together.) It's all a little joyless.

Whatever happened to that job you used to love?

How did you get to be in your current job? Was it as a result of a well-informed and balanced set of decisions made early in your career, taking into account your personal strengths, aptitudes, preferences and values, leading you down a well-supported path towards job fulfilment?

Or (possibly more likely) was it because someone made you an offer when you needed it? The money and location were right? It looked good on your CV? It was a job at least.

How often along the way have you been disappointed? Maybe the public façade is great, but behind the scenes the place is a madhouse. The job advertised bears little or no relation to the reality. Your new boss was charming at the interview but turns out to be a control freak. The job just isn't what you had hoped it would be.

I made a terrible career move once. I knew it by 9.05am on my first day. I was having my first meeting with my new boss. I'd just started as a regional manager for a chain of branded restaurants.

"Treat all your managers as lying, thieving, lazy bastards and you will never be disappointed and you may occasionally be pleasantly surprised," said my new boss. If I'd had the courage I should have got up and left right then. I didn't. I stuck it for one year, during which all my fears materialised. I eventually escaped before they could fire me. My marriage came under severe stress and at one point I started to entertain thoughts of suicide. I was probably clinically depressed – sadly, a condition which is all too common these days. I learned a very hard lesson, you might say.

Maybe you've been in your job a few years now, trying to make some sense of it. Maybe you're struggling. If you had a second chance, would you make the same decisions? What if you knew you couldn't fail: what choices would you make?

How much of your energy, talent, commitment, passion is being brought to your current job? Is your potential being truly realised?

Sorry to be so nosey. We've only just met.

If you've allowed time to answer any of these highly personal questions, how do you now feel, and what does that tell you about your feelings towards your job?

How's your career engine running?

My mojo engine started misfiring in my early thirties. This was way back in what my children call The Dark Ages, when "lunch hour" was taken with colleagues in the staff restaurant (as opposed to the directors' dining room, which was on a different floor and had a butler). I knew where the managing director was by the trail of his cigar smoke. A mobile phone was bigger and heavier than a brick, and those who weren't important enough to have one carried a device on their belt called a pager. Whenever it buzzed you'd have to drive around country lanes looking for a telephone box where the phone still worked: needle, haystack.

By then the rapid trajectory I had enjoyed since joining the drinks industry as a graduate trainee (I had an 18-month induction programme, the finest in the business, lucky me) had started to tail off. I was beginning to look at my company pension projections and see how affluent I could be if only I could stick this and complete the full 40-year service. I was bored, I didn't fit the job and it didn't fit me, and I'd say I was achieving less than half of my potential.

Being someone who prefers to avoid conflict, I did nothing about it. I'm also an eternal optimist, and I used to kid myself that things were going to get better. I had my eye on my boss's job: quite fancied his office, having a bigger car and being called a marketing director. He would get promoted soon surely, and I would be a natural successor. I hung around waiting for it to happen. Only 18 months or so. What a waste of time.

And anyway, I was wrong. He was asked to leave, they replaced him with a wild-eyed narcissist from a garden machinery manufacturer, and I got made redundant. Thank goodness. I might still be there otherwise. That well-aimed kick up the rear end woke me up and gave me the necessary nudge to sit down and think about what I really wanted to do, what my strengths were, and above all what was important. Having drifted into a career choice based on who was first to make me an offer when I graduated from university, I now had a moment to make some informed choices and try again. I got into the training world (at my wife's suggestion, to whom I am eternally grateful) and have never looked back.

Hardly a well-thought-out career plan: stumbling and bumbling about, waiting for things to get better. Which they did not. Is this something you can relate to?

How badly is the engine damaged?

Looking back, I can recognise when my engine started misfiring. How about you? Let's try to plug in our engine diagnostics software and measure any damage in some way.

Gallup's 2017 "State of the American workplace" survey of 195,000 employees revealed that only 33% of employees were actively engaged with their employment.[1] The rest were (and probably still are) either actively disengaged (16%) or neither one nor the other (51% in neutral). In his foreword to the survey, Gallup's CEO Jim Clifton urges executives to address these results by committing to changing the culture from "command and control to one of high development and coaching conversations". As we'll see later in the book, this is a massive challenge.

The survey goes on to conclude that only 21% of employees strongly agree that their performance is managed in a way that motivates them to do outstanding work. As Clifton says:

"Employees feel rather indifferent about their job and the work they are being asked to do. Organizations are not giving them compelling reasons to stay, so it should come as no surprise that most employees (91%) say the last time they changed jobs, they left their company to do so."

By the way, Gallup's 2017 "State of the global workplace" report shows only 10% of Western European employees engaged (enthusiastic about and involved) in the organisation they work in.[2]

Let me share what my own face-to-face, on-the-job research has shown me. On the majority of group training workshops I run, I do an introductory ice-breaking activity which includes a self-assessment exercise in which I ask participants to tell me how much of their working week they spend doing what I call Right Right activity – work which they feel is appropriate to their role and their function – and doing it efficiently. It's the top right quadrant on my model.

Working Smart

1. RIGHT THING WRONG APPROACH	4. RIGHT THING RIGHT APPROACH
2. WRONG THING WRONG APPROACH	3. WRONG THING RIGHT APPROACH

The answer to this, year after year and across the variety of organisations I work with around the world, is 40%. Employees are telling me that they spend only 40% of their time, or two days per week, doing the Right activity the Right way.

I repeat: two days per week. This amazingly low level of productivity ties in with the results of a 2014 Harris Poll survey on behalf of CareerBuilder in the US showing the top 10 productivity killers at work. (Use of mobile phone came in as the worst culprit.[3])

Forty per cent. Process that thought for a moment. Imagine the impact on the bottom line if it became 50%. At best this is a missed opportunity; at worst it is systemic workplace dysfunctionality along with, as one of my research respondents called it, "squandering of human capital". What a waste. And who are we to blame for it: managers or employees?

Read that last sentence again if you like. Ahem.

Examples of workplace madness are all too easy to find. The projects which misfire because no one really checked what the customer wanted. The hours of meetings with no agendas, no timings, no actions, no minutes, attended by too many (and often the wrong) people, and which therefore make little progress. People being competitive with others simply to stay ahead. Feeling they can't be themselves, that they have to put on an alternative persona when they walk in the door to the office.

All too often people transmit without the message being received. People simply do not understand what is being said (or why). Try asking someone to explain to you what the latest office mantra really means and their eyes may start to shift a bit. I've come across some great ones recently:

"Drive to digitize"

"Be the fun"

"Employee empowerment"

They sound great, but what do they *mean*?

You get my drift. The chances are, you are surrounded by workplace malfunction. Can you still see it for what it is, or is malfunction the new normal?

Introduce yourself!

It seems appropriate to include in the introduction to the book an introduction to the most fascinating person you know: *you*!

Let me invite you to introduce yourself to yourself via these questions, all of which I use regularly on the workshops I run. They tend to get to the heart of things fairly quickly, and I hope taking a few minutes to consider them properly will help get you tuned in and ready for the rest of the book.

I have a variety of techniques for getting the answers to these questions without going round the table one by one starting on the left. This is what is known by trainers like me as "Creeping Death". It raises anxiety levels in the room, no one listens because they're too busy panicking about what to say, and for the *Introverts* in the room (more on them later), it is the equivalent of inviting them to stick pins in their own eyeballs.

Here are the areas we cover – maybe jot down your own answers to what, if I were a doctor, would be me asking you to stick a thermometer in your mouth. Let's see what temperature you're running at, and remember, write down a 100% honest answer if you want to get any value from the exercise.

- Your job and how long you've been doing it
- Your first job and how much you got paid (fun item)
- The purpose of your job: what difference does it make, and why should anybody care?

- How much of your potential (as a percentage) is unlocked in your job?
- The ongoing level of stress you operate at in your job, on a 1–10 scale (10 being high)
- The two values you hold most dear
- How productive you are in your job (1–10)
- One word to describe the quality of leadership around you
- One word to describe how customers would assess your organisation
- Your proudest achievement
- The thing you are working on to develop yourself currently
- The best book you have read this year
- What you would do if you knew you couldn't fail.

If you took the time to answer these, check out how you now feel. What does that tell you?

If you didn't, what does that tell you?

Fixing the engine

If we accept that life at work is more challenging than it's ever been, let's look on the bright side. The good news is that we are not doomed. Absolutely not. Your career engine can be boosted, repaired or tuned up: it is never too late. You may not be able to fix some of the fundamental systemic workplace dysfunctionality you probably find yourself in, but you most certainly can do a lot more than you may realise to recreate and renegotiate your place within it.

And even better news: often all it requires is some quite simple changes of behaviour, many of which you already know but have forgotten, and none of which involves rocket science. Being "a bear of little brain" myself, I don't do complicated.

This book is designed to give you enough information to be able to fix your own engine. My aim is for it to be practical and feasible. It may leave you wanting to know more, which is fine. I intend to give you enough insight into the repair tools to be able to apply the fix.

I know this stuff works because I keep in touch with people I have introduced it to, and they report back on the difference it makes. You could say it's been fully road tested. When people successfully apply these tools, it is always liberating and often life changing. It's worked for thousands of people I know of over the years, and therefore I know it can work for you.

Right, enough said. Overalls on, let's get to work!

Getting the most from the book

Just before we start, let me congratulate you. You have taken the first step by buying the book and opening it.

When I was about halfway through writing it I mentioned the book to a fellow training consultant, Guy Arnold, and asked him what his top 10 tools for boosting career mojo would be. The first one he said was "be proactive". In other words, recognise when you need to change something and take the first step.

You have done precisely that. I imagine that unless you are reading the book out of pure curiosity, you want to change something. You have at the very least a work-related itch and you want to scratch it. And you have decided that this book might help you to do that. I certainly hope it will.

Let's look at how to have your investment (mainly in the time it is going to take you to read it) pay off as productively as possible.

User instructions

The main body of the book is called "Boost your mojo"! It features the top 10 tools and techniques which my face-to-face research tells me are the most beneficial in surviving and thriving in today's workplace. It is not the definitive list, others may form the content of another book. These are the ones which I believe have potential to make most change to your working life. (Oh, and by the way, lots of this material will work well at home, too. You're welcome.)

Each chapter/tool is self-contained, so you can either read them in sequence or pick out the ones with titles which appeal most. At the end of each chapter I pose some questions which I invite you to consider before moving on. In my experience it would be a good idea to write down any actions or answers to the questions as you read. Come back to them later and you will probably have lost your train of thought.

(Quick side note on that point: I know from my research that a surprisingly high number of mid-career workers do not read books. You are at least reading this one, but you might find you can derive a huge mojo boost simply from making time to read more. Seeing the world through a different set of eyes can be fascinating and therapeutic. When I started reading business books in earnest about 15 years ago, it really made a difference.)

Be realistic!

As you read, keep in mind Stephen Covey's Circle of Influence. In his book *The 7 habits of highly effective people*, Covey suggests that our best use of energy is to direct it at the Circle of Influence: things that we have the opportunity to change.[4] Directing energy into things where we have no influence (the Circle of Concern) is likely not to be productive. This is the difference between being proactive and being reactive. We cannot change the political and economic landscape, the news, the threat of terrorism or the ageing population. We can change the way we conduct ourselves in meetings, the jobs we apply for, the way we reply to an angry email. Don't put energy into fighting battles you can never win is my advice.

Practice makes perfect

When we consciously apply a model or technique, we do so using what trainers call *Conscious Competence*. You have to retrieve the model from your "modern" brain (the neocortex) and apply it deliberately. Fortunately, you don't have to do it consciously for ever. How annoying would it be to have to consciously clean your teeth every morning or think about how to reverse your car? I used to quote research which showed that for Conscious Competence to turn into Unconscious Competence (i.e. become a habit), you have to do something deliberately 27 times. This has since been superseded, I am told by a recent Psychology graduate, but nonetheless the principle holds good: practice makes perfect, and eventually you don't have to remember any more – the conscious behaviour becomes habitual. Apparently neuroscientists have a saying: "neurons that fire together, wire together." In other words, if you repeat an action, the neurons involved connect together more strongly, meaning it becomes more and more easy to do it.

Therefore, for the lessons in this book to become fully integrated and habitual, you will need to remember to apply them regularly. Think about that as you start to read. How can you make sure you remember to apply this technique? Can someone else remind you of it? Do you need to set up reminders, visually or otherwise? How can you nag yourself into a different way of behaving? Choose whatever system works for you, but be aware that you do need a system.

A couple of words of warning

I just wanted to say that nothing in this book is pure *truth*. I offer you my thoughts and suggestions for you to consider, and you may choose to use them. But none is guaranteed to deliver results (sadly, otherwise I might be very rich indeed), and there is always an alternative option. Please do not feel you have to blindly apply everything I say: the key is to exercise judgement and apply things in a balanced and thoughtful way.

Similarly, this book is not an academic treatise. It doesn't aim to say everything there is to say on any given topic, nor does it attempt to bring in all the possible perspectives. There isn't room for that – if you want to know all the angles there are plenty of other books and sources you can refer to. I hope instead you find my words a source of inspiration which leaves you curious, eager to know more and ready to have a go at applying at least some of it.

I also want to caution you against allowing it to overwhelm you. Trying to tackle too many things at the same time is likely to be less successful than changing one thing at a time. You don't have to do all of this at the same time for it to make a difference. Maybe set yourself a goal of reading one chapter per month and consciously applying one idea from it. Be realistic, and don't push yourself too hard. This book is meant to be your friend, not your taskmaster!

As with most learning, we have to know where we are starting from before we can progress. I ask you to be as honest with yourself as you can and open yourself up to self-critique. Only then can you build. It might be helpful occasionally to check out your self-perception with someone else. Where you see yourself as having a strength, they may disagree. Learning starts with self-awareness, so be ready to test your own perceptions. That may be uncomfortable at times, but that's OK. Embrace that feeling! "No pain = no gain", as we trainer types are sometimes heard to say.

A heads up on the content

After I have set out the landscape as I see it in Section 1, the main body of the book is in Section 2, where I introduce the 10 tools my research tells me you'll find most useful. Warning: Section 1 does not make for particularly easy reading: it paints a gloomy picture of the state of the nation as I see it. Please don't let it get you too despondent. We are not all doomed, and my whole reason for writing this book is that there are plenty of ways to make more of the opportunities available to us in our day-to-day efforts in the workplace. So just grit your teeth and see how much of what I see is in line with your experience.

In Section 2 the mood lightens: trust me on that. I'll share the top 10 tools you can use to transform your workplace reality. These are:

1. **Reset your compass.** Defining a "why" for yourself and the team, how to understand where you fit and what the priorities are, setting team goals.

2. **Build more trust.** Why trust is so weak, how this impacts us, why trust is the first part of win/win, how to build it (the CORE model of trust, see page 63), the controlled disclosure and vulnerability concept, how you need to set aside time for it and plan it.

3. **Get out of the playground.** What Parents, Adults and Children look like at work, how we can inadvertently create Parents and Children, what to do when others treat us as Children, how to get Parents to become Adults.

4. **Invest in relationships.** What you need to know in order to do your job well, how to have a constructive one-to-one with your boss, sharing personality profiles and how to use that information, proposing meaningful and motivating

objectives, knowing what information to share and how. Invest time in key players. Empathy, humanity, emotional intelligence, coaching and helping others to be their best.

5. **Negotiate for yourself.** Why we need to say no, why we don't (our mental limits), how to say it without damaging the relationship, how to turn it into a negotiation using creativity, use of the "if" word, nothing for nothing, work out your assertiveness level, how doing it well builds relationships.

6. **Avoid avoidance.** How to find win/win by exposing shared interests and needs, seeking first to understand, slowing down your response, what to do if it becomes emotional, why avoidance is usually a bad idea, understanding your conflict-handling preference (the Thomas-Kilmann model, see page 120).

7. **Listen more, transmit less.** How information is power, how to use this when negotiating, great questions to ask to help you understand others' positions, how to use this to resolve conflict, how it builds empathy, the power of silence, how this is welcomed by Introverts.

8. **Think!** Getting more done by slowing down, things to check at the beginning, the importance of Process, how to help others not go down the wrong road, great questions to ask.

9. **Meet intelligently.** The amount of time wasted by bad meetings, the "no agenda = no meeting" principle, how to build an agenda that works, minutes and clear action planning, how to continuously improve meetings, recognising when to facilitate and not have an opinion, how to produce clarity and focus for discussion.

10. **Know yourself.** Myers-Briggs® preferences and how they impact the way you see the world and function at work. Reading and respecting others' preferences, rapport, how what you think good looks like will not be the same for others, how to respect and adapt to Introversion or Extraversion.

After explaining each tool, I have a few simple but deep questions for you. Try to take some time to think about them before you say "how interesting" and move on to the next one. Spending time to force yourself to think (and make some notes, I suggest) really could pay dividends.

Section 3 deals with what to do if really the right thing to do is to leave, and Section 4 looks at how to maintain your career mojo once you've got it running sweetly.

At the back of the book are some endnotes with details of all the resources I refer to. A small number embedded in the text indicates an endnote. I have done my best to accredit all my sources, but any omissions are entirely unintentional and will be rectified when we reprint.

How much do you want it?

Finally, before we jump in, I have a question for you: How much do you want to change?

These words do not, unfortunately, come with a sachet of magic dust secreted in the back cover. Sprinkle it on your hair and it will transform your career mojo. If only it did, I reckon I could charge a lot more for it.

The only person who can decide to apply these changes is you, and you will do so only if you decide to (kind of obvious, I guess). You are going to need to want to use the new approach, you will need to believe it, it will need to tie in with your personal value system, with your longer-term goals and with your sense of who you are, before you are even half likely to make any sort of change.

This book is designed to put the ideas out there in an accessible and pragmatic way, so that you can then make your choices. The rest is up to you. I sincerely hope it helps.

Section 1
Diagnose your engine

"The world is not just rapidly changing: it is being dramatically reshaped. It is starting to operate differently in many realms at once. And this reshaping is happening faster than we have yet been able to reshape ourselves, our leadership, our institutions, our societies, and our ethical choices."

Dov Seidman[5]

Before we start

As I wrote this book I sent out bits of it to people I knew would give me honest feedback. One such is James Robertson, who is a business writer who runs a systems analysis consultancy called Atlantic Systems Guild. I sent him this chapter and he soon wrote back:

> *"God, that was depressing. I understand your need to set the stage, and if we are to be realistic, the state of things is depressing. F!£$ing depressing."*

Because he knows how to give clear and constructive feedback (he's a Kiwi, they're better at that than softy Brits like me), he then went on to suggest how I could balance out the chapter a bit, which I hope I have done.

But the fact remains, this chapter might be a bit gloomy because I have not pulled any punches. No point trying to dress up bad news. As my old trainer friend Jeff Delay used to say: "You can't polish a turd." I'm not aiming to be alarmist, and I'm not trying to overstate anything. I realise that when you lay out everything that is happening on the same table, it can paint a gloomy picture. Please bear with me on this. We have to know where we're starting from and it may be no bad thing to see it for what it is.

Bear in mind, though, that this book is based on the proposition that you can make a huge difference to your own situation if you choose to, and it aims to show you how. It'll be alright.

An optimist's opinion

I'm a natural optimist. To the point of naivety, those that know me would say. If in doubt, I give the benefit of the doubt. I trust others quickly, I anticipate reciprocation when I do favours, and I bumble along expecting that things will work out fine, just you wait and see.

But I can't help feeling uneasy about the state of today's workplace. I spend much of my time face to face with groups of mid-career people behind closed doors working on ways to help them cope with the pressures that are bearing down on them. Actually, they're not just bearing down, they're bearing up on them from below, and in from the sides. Whichever way you look at it, people are being squeezed. Hard. I can't help but conclude (and remember, this is an optimist talking) that the "squeezed middle", a phrase used by British politicians but which I like to borrow, has never had it so bad. And it's going to get worse, not better. Sorry.

I put it to you that your career mojo engine may be malfunctioning in various ways, owing in part to what is going on in a world that is changing faster than ever and to some people appears to be going mad.

Let's take a look under the bonnet to see what's going on. Make a note of the malfunctions you recognise.

Internal dysfunctionality from above

In the last couple of years I have started to make note of the examples I hear from people talking about the internal dysfunctionality they have to deal with which flows downhill from above. Here's a representative sample:

"People are continuously being asked to do more with less, and this has been happening for years now. It's not sustainable." (Note: 43% of teachers, 81% of senior doctors and 66% of nurses say they are considering leaving their profession in the UK, and the most frequently cited reason is the stress caused by increasing managerial demands.)

"The only training I got was mandatory product training. This compromised my personal values of lifelong learning. When on top of that I started to feel no connection with the message, I knew I had to leave."

"Priorities keep changing, and we have to run with the latest buzzwords. We don't know where we're going, and I'm not clear what's needed from me."

"I see my peers struggling every day with being stuck in the rut of too many emails, too many meetings, no raises, no manager reviews, no time for skills improvement, starting the next two programs before the last one is finished and feeling like there is no way out or forward."

"I was a hamster on its wheel. The number one tool for survival is take care of yourself because no one is going to say 'no' or 'stop' on your behalf."

"There seems to be plenty of excitement at the top, but in the middle people are just scared."

"The anxiety is intense. There's a lack of clarity, and it's all so complicated. Because the pace is so fast, people don't have time to talk, and they're afraid to. There's no pausing. It's exhausting."

"We have made it too easy to get hold of each other, and you feel a constant need to respond."

"Managers don't want us acting out of our silos, so that it's easier to track who is doing what, and who's accountable. They talk Agile, but don't get it."

"The company doesn't love me. If you've been around 10 years or more, you're old. They don't performance manage you, they just have to replace you."

"Sometimes it's an uphill battle – just when I think I've aligned with someone's strengths and built the trust needed for open and honest collaboration, management shifts gears/priorities/deliverables/firefights (you name it) and pulls the rug right out from under the best-laid plans."

Another one I often hear when working in Europe is the intense level of micromanagement that is perpetrated by US-led companies. Tony works in sales operations in the UK and tells me "you can't breathe unless you do it in the way ordered by HQ in the US. There's also the 'not invented here syndrome' prevalent among US-led organisations – a complete failure to understand how much good stuff can come from outside the US."

Many managers express frustration at the short-term thinking in their organisations. As companies try to make each quarter's results better than the last, the focus increases on short-term results and proper mid-term planning becomes a rarity.

Mark Abell is a director at sales and service consultancy Imparta. Through his work with clients of all shapes and sizes he sees the results for himself.

"With reduced workforce numbers and a bigger squeeze on productivity, there is less time for people to think deeply and create new things. The doing becomes everything – time to really think through a problem or opportunity is rare indeed."

In his book *Think: why crucial decisions can't be made in the blink of an eye*, Michael LeGault talks about stress levels.[6]

"The rise of 'stress', or rather the symptoms of stress, in contemporary society is a sign not only that more people are in difficult situations, but tellingly, that they are unable to respond to or think their way out of these situations. It is a sign, ultimately, that more people are having trouble taking charge of their lives. Today, stress and its co-conspirator, so-called information overload, are two major factors in the weakening of mental energy needed to do creative, technical work and solve everyday problems. It is why so many people say they are in perpetual 'crisis mode' and have the feeling that their lives are 'out of control'. It is why some are falling off the side of their mountain."

He wrote his book in 2006. Of course, things have improved dramatically since then. Only kidding. More than 12 years later, I fear things have got much worse.

These are not isolated examples. I've tried to show you the range and depth of the concerns people express. Other sources of frustration include the directive style of management people use (often as a means supposedly of increasing speed) and not receiving coaching (as we'll see later, this is a major negative), or indeed having quality time of any sort with managers.

Pressure from below

There is no doubt that mid-career workers feel pressure from the younger generation. Millennials have a different attitude towards the demands for speed and agility, largely because they know no different. As part of my research for this book I carried out a survey of 300 or so folks I have trained over the years, and one of the biggest concerns I picked up was that mid-careerers worry about how to stay relevant and develop the skills they need to do so. Some expressed concern about whether they need to reinvent themselves, and if so whether they are capable of it.

As Eric "Astro" Teller, CEO of Google's X research and development lab, puts it:

"What we are experiencing today, with shorter and shorter innovation cycles and less and less time to adapt, is the difference between a constant state of destabilization versus occasional destabilization."[7] *If the millennials are able to ride this roller coaster better than the rest, it adds to the sense of unease which many mid-careerers may feel.*

As Stephen Covey puts it in his book *The speed of trust*:

"Technology and globalization are outdating skill sets faster than ever before. The half-life of our current knowledge and skills is much shorter than it ever has been, and suddenly someone who was very competent and even had a great track record in yesterday's world may no longer be competent in today's world."[8]

As if that wasn't bad enough, from what I hear the Millennials are themselves becoming increasingly disgruntled. Maybe their job isn't delivering on what they expected, or they are feeling taken advantage of. Certainly there seems to be an increasing tension between them and the older generation, leading to mutual suspicion and mistrust. The Millennials feel very strongly about this, as I detected in the focus groups I ran while researching this book. The level of passion and outspokenness was much higher with the Millennial groups than with others. Either this indicates more depth of feeling, or maybe it's just that the older folks have become weary of it all and given up pushing back. Anyway, Millennial malaise adds further to the pressure on the mid-careerers because they often manage these people.

Pressure from outside

We live in remarkable times. American journalist and author Thomas Friedman describes this moment as "a fundamental turning point in history". His book *Thank you for being late* shows how technology, globalisation and climate change are developing at rapidly increasing speeds, in ways which are fundamentally changing our environment.[9] Maybe it really is a turning point.

Why might it be such a big moment? Well, for a start, the middle ground appears to have lost its voice, and extremism and tribalism have asserted themselves in various guises, most notably with political upheaval across Europe and the US, which is no longer the dominating force across the world and appears to have lost its self-confidence. Trust levels in politicians there have collapsed to an all-time low. China increasingly appears to be in the driving seat, with unknown agendas of its own. People may be feeling physically insecure, culturally insecure and economically insecure, all at the same time.

Technology is a huge driver of uncertainty, of course. Artificial intelligence is already taking over jobs, many in areas we would have thought impossible five years ago. The driverless car is already being tested, as are the surgeonless medical operation, the lawyerless court case and many others. Workers in a UK insurance company have been offered enhanced redundancy terms now if they identify that their role could be done by a machine within five years. A research study at Oxford University in 2013 concluded that 47% of American jobs are at risk of being taken over by computers in the next two decades. This is supported by McKinsey, which studied 2,000 work activities in more than 800 different occupations and concluded that 45% of them could be automated by currently proven and tested technologies. Furthermore, 60% of all occupations could see 30% of their activities being automated.[10]

I'm seeing it for myself. I stayed recently in a hotel in San Jose, California, and as I walked into reception a machine shaped like a small dustbin rolled across the lobby and parked itself in a docking station. Curious to know more, I found a small menu of snack items available from this new room service assistant. I had to try it. I rang the number, ordered a Twix (I know how to live the good life) and waited. Five minutes later my phone rang and an automated voice told me my delivery was here. I went to the door and as I opened it, the dustbin beeped sweetly at me and lit up its blue plastic lid. There inside was my Twix, which I retrieved according to the instructions on the screen. It had to check whether there was anything else it could help me with and ask for some immediate feedback before peeping me goodbye and trundling off to get into the lift, which miraculously arrived when it stood itself next to the call button. A small example, but what will that technology allow the hotel to automate over the next few years?

The Bank of England's chief economist Andy Haldane estimated in 2015 that 15 million British jobs are at risk of automation, as are 80 million in the US.[11] How society will respond to this comprehensive reshaping of the workplace is a "known unknown", as former US Secretary of Defense Donald Rumsfeld might have put it.

Forget the "digital divide": that's soon going to disappear. Soon virtually everyone on the planet will have a device and an internet connection. The divide will be what futurist writer Marina Gorbis describes as a "motivational divide": who has the self-motivation, agility, willingness to learn and persistence to keep learning for the rest of their lives, *and who does not.*[12]

As much as 50% of the content of your university degree may be obsolete within five years, according to business strategist Heather McGowan. "Hard-won monolithic degrees earned early in life could be obsolete within a decade – well before the debt incurred to secure that degree is repaid and the investment realized." Oh dear. She goes on to make a crucial point about how to survive in this age of accelerations: "Learning becomes more important than knowing … the new killer skill set is an agile mindset that values learning over knowing."[13]

My own research has shown that one of the things mid-career workers are most worried about is how they can remain relevant and acquire the skills needed in the moment. How do you figure out what you need to learn, let alone how to go about learning it?

For many people, the outside world is tougher than ever and becoming a little scary. And we haven't even mentioned Mother Nature yet.

I'm a baby boomer, born in 1958. I have seen the world's population double from 3 billion in 1958 to 6 billion in 1999. If I keep walking the dog and eating plenty of yoghurt, I could see it triple, up to 9.7 billion in 2050. Think of the pressure on resources, especially as these people are going to be moving to large urban areas and consuming water, electricity and lots of protein. Are we going to be able to keep up with the demand for jobs? According to Adair Turner, chairman of the Institute for New Economic Thinking, yes and no.[14]

An essay published in 2015 on international media organisation Project Syndicate suggests that population growth in Europe, Russia and Japan is manageable because of low fertility rates. However, in other places, such as West Africa, it is far from manageable. Between 1950 and 2050 Uganda's population will have increased 20-fold and Niger's 30-fold. Turner believes: "The resulting high unemployment, particularly of young men, could foster political instability … The European Union could be facing a wave of migration that makes debates about accepting hundreds of thousands of asylum seekers seem irrelevant."

Social unrest looks like it is here to stay. Here is what Stephen Hawking says about it:

"The automation of factories has already decimated jobs in traditional manufacturing, and the rise of artificial intelligence is likely to extend this job destruction deep into the middle classes, with only the most caring, creative or supervisory roles remaining. This in turn will accelerate the already widening economic inequality around the world. The internet and the platforms that it makes possible allow very small groups of individuals to make enormous profits whilst employing very few people. This is inevitable, it is progress, but it is also socially destructive."[15]

A radio feature I was half listening to this very morning stated that if you were born after 2012 there are half as many animal species on Earth as there were if you were born before 1970.

All this adds up to what some refer to as VUCA: Volatility, Uncertainty, Complexity and Ambiguity. None of which is helpful for knowing what you're supposed to be doing, what's important or where you're headed. Not good for business, not conducive to investment, and certainly not good for the employee. With such an uncertain climate at a macro level, businesses become more cautious, trust levels go down, and employees can feel less confident about their careers and less secure in their jobs.

The typical mid-career worker may feel increasingly stuck. Not confident in making a career move, and not having the ability to take the risk anyway, with a mortgage and young children to fend for. Many have not had a decent pay rise for years, driven by another external pressure, the financial meltdown of 2008, from which recovery has been slow and fragile.

Added to the political and financial uncertainty is the gradual erosion in societal norms driven by the incessant growth in the use of social media. It's making us miserable and causing a breakdown in meaningful relationships. Swiss author Rolf Dobelli puts it this way: "Never in the history of mankind have so many people compared themselves with others, and that causes misery. Then it cuts your attention into so many short pieces that we have lost the ability to stay focused on one train of thought for longer than a minute, which has very strong implications on the intellectual life of someone; debating issues becomes not a question of argument any more but little tweets. We've never been more connected, and we've never been more isolated."[16]

Research shows we touch, swipe or tap our phones 2,617 times a day. No wonder we can't focus properly any more. We're addicted. In 2015, Boston Consulting Group published research into how people use their phones – 38% said they'd give up sex for a year rather than give up their mobile phone.[17] I kid you not.

And because we're on email via our phones, the length of our working day has gone up from seven and a half hours to nine and a half. Despite this, productivity hasn't improved at all, which means we're wasting time (28% of each day on email, for a start). We're still expected to be at our desks all that time, and the result is that we're tired and stressed. In his podcast "Eat Sleep Work Repeat", Bruce Daisley, Twitter's European Vice President, says: "Half of all workers show signs of exhaustion. There's a constant sense that you never complete anything."

Probably because we're all mucking about on Twitter, Bruce.

Using the wrong components

Finally (you may be relieved to read – we can all put up with only so much doom and gloom), let's ask whether we may have career mojo malfunction because we are using the wrong engine components.

I use a survey tool on many of the courses I run where people complete an assessment of the team they spend most time with and the results give a score against each of eight characteristics of a high-performance team. You can use it to diagnose your own team if you like: here's the link https://myjobisntworking.com/docs/Team-Assessment.pdf.

Over the years, one of the bottom three has consistently been "Processes and Procedures". This comes out as a significant time waster. Trying to work out how to use a particular tool, getting it to use the right data, or indeed being forced to use it when a much slicker tool would have been a phone call: these cause a lot of angst and malfunction. Even when you do pick up a phone, it can be hard to get an answer. I was with a supply chain manager in China recently who told me she had spent one whole day trying to figure out who the owner of a particular non-functioning internal tool was. "It's enough to make you want to cry," she told me.

When I ask why people haven't done something to fix these time wasters, the usual answer is "It's not mine to fix" or "I tried and gave up because it wasn't worth the hassle." Slightly more worrying is the comment some make that "making a suggestion for improvement is seen as troublemaking". All of these sound to me like good excuses for conflict avoidance, which we'll come on to later in the book. Maybe it is time to revisit the battles we have given up on and sort them out once and for all.

The other thing I see with worn-out processes and procedures is that people don't fix them because they don't get round to reviewing them and learning from mistakes. They listen to the squeaky brakes and just keep on topping up with brake fluid rather than replacing the leaky brake pipe. According to a 2014 survey, the average US employee spends 45% of their working day doing their real job. The rest of the day is spent wading through email and attending pointless meetings. Many employees have extended their working day so they can stay late to do their "real job".

Sometimes it's not the tool that's wrong, it's the way it's used. A classic about which I hear no end of moans is the annual performance review. This is often used as the one occasion when a manager sits down and gives the reviewee some feedback, and it can be a demotivating experience rather than a constructive and motivational one. Managers do not

prepare adequately, they lack the skills to use the opportunity to its full potential and the reviewee gets little out of it.

For a little light relief at this point, take a look at a short video I made with my old friend and colleague, Spencer Holmes (https://youtu.be/rQPfHP2rziE). It is 12 minutes of unadulterated corporate dysfunctionality, in which I have an appraisal meeting with Spencer. It is full of deliberate errors. See how many you can spot. If you want to know what we think the deliberate errors are, email me (michael@reallearningforachange.com) and I'll send you our list.

Run well, this annual meeting can and should be a motivating and productive session, creating clarity and allowing strengths to be utilised and potential to be unlocked. It is often the opposite. As someone once said to me, "We have a forced ranking system for our reviews (i.e. a pre-established quota for how many of each ranking each manager is allowed to award rather than awarding purely on merit) and it sucks. It's basically like handing out candy if your face fits. If you're not in the inner circle, forget it (and in my case, being an expat, my face was never going to be in the inner circle)."

No wonder the annual appraisal meeting really is one that can fill both parties with dread.

Yes, you can find your own way around this!

I hope this chapter hasn't been too tough to read. I don't think I've overstated it, and I suspect I haven't pointed out anything you weren't aware of. But maybe you have lost sight of the big picture and this has crept up on you slightly unawares. Sorry if that's a bit of a rude awakening.

There's no dodging the fact that today's workplace is really challenging – arguably the trickiest it's ever been. I'm certainly glad I went self-employed 10 years ago and am able to decide for myself how to adapt. When I look back to my life in a large corporate in the 1980s, it's fair to say in retrospect that while we didn't know it at the time, we never had it so good.

If you recognise that your mojo might be running slow because of some of the themes I've touched on, that's great news in a way. Now you can start to do something about it. You probably can't do a lot to stop the pressure, but you absolutely can devise strategies to deal with it more effectively. Simple changes have the potential to transform your journey through all of this.

That is what the rest of the book is about: the 10 tools I know people like you find most useful in helping them survive and thrive within the tough reality. When I work with people and introduce these tools, I have hard evidence (because they tell me when I follow up with them) that this stuff works.

I often comment to people that I can literally see the difference it has made on their faces. I can think of one recent example, where someone applied the first tool in the next section of the book, and when we next spoke the difference in his energy level was palpable. He had been asking himself what the point of his job was and was contemplating leaving the company. Now he has a real purpose and has fundamentally rethought what is required of him as a leader. His passion is back, he's having fun, and he has something to get up for in the morning. I could feel it even though I was 500 miles away. People with well-functioning career mojos are usually easy to spot.

"We are where we are," one of my favourite phrases. No point wasting energy analysing or moaning about why things are the way they are. It is what it is.

I hope you're ready now to get on and boost your career mojo.

Notes

- Make a note here of the malfunctions you recognise.

- What particular pressures are you under?

- Which causes the most damage to your mojo?

Section 2
Boost your mojo!

Tool 1. Reset your compass

*"If you don't know where you are going,
any road will get you there."*
Lewis Carroll, Alice in Wonderland

You've worked here for 40,000 years...
so how long have you had these 'doubts'?

Introduction

This chapter/tool comes with a health warning. I think it is the most challenging of my 10 mojo repair tools because it asks you to consider some profound questions which may have no easy answer or which may produce answers that rock you a bit. I hope that's OK. We have to tackle this one as it is the source of so much mid-career misery in the workplace.

Too many folks who have worked more than a couple of years have lost sight of what's important. They are not sure which direction they are heading in, even though they may feel it is no longer the right one for them. If you are one of those people this chapter aims to act as a wake-up call and to encourage you to get your bearings, work out where you want to go and reset the compass accordingly. And if you think you are pretty clear on this, use the chapter to sanity check and make sure there aren't any pieces missing.

Remember: you always have a choice. You can choose your attitude. If you choose to try to improve your working environment, you have a chance of success. If you choose to believe that everything around you cannot be changed and that you are powerless, I guarantee your brain will allow you to prove yourself right. Anorexic people only ever see a fat person in the mirror. As you work through the chapter, keep checking in with yourself and ask what you can learn from your response to what I am suggesting.

Suggestion: if this chapter starts to become a bit heavy going, take a break and come back to it.

"What's the point?"

There is nothing more dispiriting than grinding away at work when you can't see the point. In the UK, according to a YouGov poll, 37% of respondents think their job makes no meaningful contribution to the world.[18] Not all of us are lucky enough to have jobs that are inherently worthwhile or that evidently contribute to the sum of human happiness, but unless you can find a meaningful point to what you do and how it makes a difference, chances are you are not going to contribute your best. At the most extreme, people devoid of purpose deteriorate both mentally and physically, as many a long-term prisoner or even retiree will no doubt attest. Today's knowledge workers are looking for meaningful and rewarding work, and are becoming increasingly demanding about the freedom they have to achieve the job's purpose.

Gallup provides us with further depressing statistics on this from its 2017 State of the American Workplace survey:[19]

- 22% of employees strongly agree their leaders have a clear direction for the organisation.
- 15% of employees strongly agree their leaders make them enthusiastic about the future.
- 13% of employees strongly agree their leaders communicate effectively with the rest of the organisation.

It doesn't look too good, does it?

A few years ago I had dinner with a manager in a large organisation who had lost her career mojo. She was weighing up what to do about this, since she knew that doing nothing was no longer an option.

"I've come to realise that I have been trying to put my heart and soul into something I find it hard to get excited about. At the end of the day, the best I am going to do is to somehow enhance a customer's invoicing experience. That does not in itself light my fire."

People who are motivated perform better, which is why organisations spend so much on extrinsic motivators – bonuses, awards ceremonies, workplace relaxation devices and so on. Motivation that comes from within – intrinsic motivation – is equally important; people who can't see the point of their work will never be intrinsically motivated.

Researcher Ken Thomas wrote about this in his book *Intrinsic motivation at work*.[20] He breaks motivation into four components: meaningfulness, choice, competence and progress. As he wrote to me recently: "Those are the things that make one experience the work task as enjoyable and rewarding."

I want to concentrate on just the first of these – meaningfulness.

Define meaningfulness for yourself and others

I often ask people on my leadership courses a simple question: "What is your purpose?"

They usually answer with "to hit my target", "to ensure continuity of supply", "to launch new products successfully". In other words, they tell me what they do. But not what the point of it is.

In his book *Start with why*, Simon Sinek offers this profound but simple insight into human behaviour:[21]

"People don't buy what you do, they buy why you do it."

Typical corporate communication starts with describing WHAT the organisation does. "We make the best batteries in the world." "We have the lowest-priced rooms in town." The trouble is, when you do that, it's often forgettable and leads the listener to say, "So what? Why should I care?"

Sinek goes on to say that compelling and inspirational communication starts with WHY, followed by HOW and then WHAT. He calls his model The Golden Circle.

THE GOLDEN CIRCLE

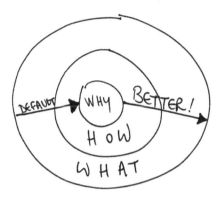

He uses Apple as an example, as they happen to be good at this, and most people get what they try to do. This is how they communicate:

"Everything we do, we believe in challenging the status quo. We believe in thinking differently.

(WHY)

The way we challenge the status quo is by making our products beautifully designed, simple to use and user-friendly.

(HOW)

We happen to make great computers."

(WHAT)

Too many organisations do this the other way round. They tell the world how great they are (WHAT they do) and maybe HOW they achieve it, but they rarely go on to define WHY they do it. This is uninspiring and does not cause others to follow.

To see Sinek explaining this model, take a look at his TED talk if you haven't already: www.ted.com/talks/simon_sinek_how_great_leaders_inspire_action. Well worth 20 minutes of your time.

Let's bring this back to you. Defining your own WHY may be a missing part in your career mojo engine. Maybe you used to know what it was and have lost sight of it. Maybe it was never there in the first place.

Many people I have met over the years haven't got a WHY. I know because in most of the workshops I run I ask them to self-assess on three questions, where 10 is high in all of them:

How productive are you? Average answer = 7 nudging 6.

How stressed are you? Average answer = 7.

How much of your potential is unlocked in your current role? Average answer = 6 nudging 7.

This is hard data from thousands of people. It tells a story of averageness. It's not life threatening, and it's no doubt sustainable, and the organisation can get by on these levels. But it is not high performance and it is certainly not job fulfilment or high motivation.

Let's come to a tricky question, dear reader. What is your WHY? The answer to this is what gets you out of bed in the morning, and why anyone else should care about what you do. If you can find a WHY for yourself, it will release energy you did not know you had. If you can get others around you to get behind it, they will follow you "with blood, sweat and tears", to quote Sinek again.

There are numerous well-known examples of people with a strong WHY – take President John F. Kennedy. JFK was visiting NASA headquarters for the first time, in 1961. While touring the facility, he introduced himself to a cleaner who was mopping the floor and asked him what he did at NASA. The cleaner replied, "I'm helping put a man on the moon!"

I often work with groups on this question, asking them to define a WHY for themselves and their teams. Possibly the best example I ever heard was a finance director of a small technology company, whose WHY was "making finance easy". Every decision he and his team have to make is now assessed against how much easier it will make life for their colleagues in the business. Once you have this clear reference point, not only will it produce clarity for others, it will also make decisions easier and release energy in the team. It gives everyone something to aim at.

What meaning can you find in your work? What if, from my earlier example, you are being asked to give your life over to improving your customer invoicing experience? Where's the personal meaning in that? I would bring it back to what I am able to influence. I can't influence the basic function of my department, but I can influence the way we work within it. Maybe I can use my experience to help others to learn and that can become my WHY. Maybe I can use this as an opportunity to learn new skills and meet new people and that can become my WHY. Maybe I can take on a project to reduce the amount of time wasted on mistakes so that no one has to give up their weekend fixing problems any more.

Whatever it is you come up with (and bear in mind this might be an activity you want to share with your team members), and however clunky it might feel initially, remember that having some sort of WHY will make a huge difference. The majority of people I have met over the years have never considered this question and as a result are missing out on a big boost to their career mojos.

I first came across *Start with why* in 2015. When I first read it, I had a big "Aha!" moment. I now realised why since becoming a coach and trainer I have so much more energy than I ever did when working in sales and marketing in the hospitality business. I spent 14 years in my earlier work life basically attempting to climb the career ladder as quickly as possible. Looking back, I did have a WHY of sorts: it was to earn as much as I could so I could afford the mortgage and our kids' education. Not much of a motivator, and not what you would call meaningful.

However, since I moved into my current world of learning and developing people, my WHY has emerged. It goes something like this:

"I believe everyone has far more potential than they realise, and the best thing I can do is help them to unlock it. This is important and worthwhile, and it can change lives. I do that by providing space and encouragement for people to learn. I happen to deliver workshops and personal coaching as a medium for this to occur."

I love my work, have never been more fulfilled, and feel privileged to do it. I discovered my WHY after the event, but it still works. It can work for you, too.

Understanding where you fit

Knowing how you contribute to the wider success can make a huge difference to your sense of motivation and purpose: to your meaningfulness. I have met too many people who do not really know where they fit in the big picture and this lies at the heart of their loss of mojo. It can also cause serious malfunction, as in this example sent to me by David Parkinson, a trainer and coach I've worked with many times:

"Some years ago a senior police staff member with the Metropolitan Police in London shared how, when she started her career, she was required to process cards

which came into the office, bearing crime details. There were thousands of cards and the job was simple data entry and mind-numbingly boring. A number of cards were short on detail or were unreadable, and for these she decided it was easiest to categorise them as 'bicycle crime'. It was some months later that she was told a government minister wanted to know why cycle crime had increased significantly, as he was preparing a House of Commons written answer."

If this sounds a bit like your own situation, then there is only one person who is responsible for taking action to change things. I think we both know who I'm talking about!

Maybe you haven't got round to asking. Perhaps you don't think it's important. Trust me on this one: it is.

Not knowing how your contribution fits within the organisation could lead to:

- **Not knowing what's important.** If you don't know what's important, how can you prioritise? If you can't prioritise, you have to treat everything as equally important, in which case you will probably burn out because you don't know what to say no to. You end up working in a land of "spray and pray", wielding a fire hose of activity and hoping some of what you do is seen as relevant.

- **Not being able to collaborate.** If you don't know what others around you are trying to achieve, it is hard to collaborate. You all end up in silos, tucked away in your cubicle, not sharing, not communicating, and probably wasting time and duplicating effort.

- **Not being seen as relevant.** This is one of the biggest fears of mid-career workers. I would argue that if they don't find out where they fit, they have only themselves to blame if they get overlooked for that promotion. It's called knowing your market. Products that don't keep abreast of the market soon go out of date.

Am I talking about you? If so, what can you do about it?

No rocket science required. Here are some practical steps you could take immediately:

1. **Check your job description.** Please don't tell me you don't have one. If you don't, again, whose fault is that? Do something about it: write it and get it approved as far up the food chain as you can go, and make sure HR are involved. If you do have one, check that it is still up to date and reflects what you do. Job descriptions are both negotiable and organic. They rarely remain valid for longer than one year, so get into the habit of reviewing them annually (possibly at your annual review.) Think also about including responsibilities within this document, which is more likely to include outcomes ("develop skills within the team", "identify new market opportunities").

2. **Ask to see your boss's job description.** I'll talk more about this in the next chapter, but for now let's recognise that if you know what your boss is measured on, you already have a sense of what is important to her. Chances are she will value efforts you make that help her deliver on her key metrics.

3. **Find out your organisation's strategy.** Decide how high level to go with this. It may be best to aim at your function's strategy rather than the organisation's as a whole, as this will be lower level and therefore more concrete. You should be able to articulate the top three things the organisation is seeking to achieve this year. Ask the relevant person to do this for you: it will have the spin-off benefit of raising your profile and it may be seen as a useful question to have asked.

4. **Map out your stakeholder landscape.** I'll talk more about this in Tool 5, but for now start by making a list of the top 10 people you need to engage with or who are impacted by what you do. Put them in some sort of order if you can, based on how influential they are in you achieving your goals and how important you are to them achieving theirs. It would be a great idea to have a discussion with them about this, and a brilliant way of building these key relationships.

When you have done all this, give yourself a pat on the back. You have made a great step forward in understanding where you fit, and in so doing you will be able to prioritise much better and relax a little, knowing that what you are doing is relevant. And along the way you will have had some interesting interactions with some key people, who may be curious to know what prompted you to do it.

Getting clarity for your co-workers

"There's nothing so wasteful as doing effectively what should not be done at all."

Anon

You work with other people in the organisation. I imagine this is in a team, or perhaps you would describe it as a group. Possibly you have roles within several teams, either as leader or team member.

How clear are these working groups about what they are aiming to achieve? If, as often happens, they are unclear, chances are it is unfulfilling, frustrating and possibly a waste of a great deal of time.

Whatever your role within these entities, you can help provide the clarity they need. This will be good for you and good for them. A team that is clear on what it is seeking to achieve will have potential to perform at an optimal level. Without that clarity it can only produce mediocre results.

There is no shortage of verbiage around teamwork, and writers over the years have produced pages of content around words such as Mission, Vision, Goals, Objectives, Targets. Often these get confused and people are not clear about which one they mean. That leads to conflict later on when people misinterpret. Let's have a go at some simple working definitions before looking at how you can work with a team on each.

Vision. This is a statement about the future you want to create. It is a vision, not a prophecy, and should create a sense of what could be. NASA: *"Put a man on the moon by the end of the decade."* Unilever: *"To make sustainable living commonplace."*

Mission. A short description of the reason the team exists. It needs to be clear, memorable and concise. Unilever: *"To add vitality to life. We meet everyday needs for nutrition, hygiene and personal care with brands that help people feel good, look good and get more out of life."*

Goals. Our aspirations for what we are going to achieve. These will align with the Mission and Vision statements. *"Attract and retain the best employees in the market."*

Objectives. The specific and measurable initiatives the team will undertake to achieve its goals. These enable the team to track its progress and know whether it has achieved what it set out to do. *"We will implement a waste-reduction programme by the end of June across all sites."*

Targets. The specific measures of activity we plan to carry out in order to meet our objectives. If we hit our targets, we deliver on the Objectives. *"Contact five new customers per day and close two deals per week for the next three months."*

It is amazing to see how often people confuse goals and objectives – you only have to Google "examples of business objectives" to see how often people are quoting what are objectives when describing goals. The same applies to Targets versus Objectives and Mission versus Vision statements.

Spending time working with a team to define these will produce a handsome return. When I facilitate sessions on this topic with teams, I use a very simple three-step process. You can work it through in a morning and then move on to defining the statements afterwards. Here's the process. You just answer these three questions and capture the output:

1. Where do we want to be? (Our vision for the future)

2. Where are we now? (What is our current reality?)

3. How do we get there? (What steps can we take to achieve the vision? What, by whom, by when?)

Be clear about what's important to you

Another regular cause of mojo damage is when people lose sight of what's important to them. What attracted them to the job in the first place has been lost somehow. Or it may have changed: starting a family, for example, often triggers a shift in priorities. Having more personal time so you can see your children grow up is the most obvious example.

Let's use this moment to run through a checklist of important questions that may help you to retune your mojo. Take your time over this. I urge you to write down your responses.

- **Values:** What are my core values that I cherish most deeply? When are they most obvious to me?

- **Alignment:** How do my values align with the organisation's espoused values? What about the organisation's real values? How often am I in conflict over this?

- **Purpose:** Do I have a clear purpose?

- **Pride:** How proud am I of what I do?

- **Persistence:** How well do I follow through on what I say I'm going to do?

It may help to discuss this with someone you trust.

I believe Values is the most important of these. When your values are different to someone else's, you are in a conflict situation, which can be difficult or perhaps impossible to resolve.

> I was speaking recently with someone who is an internal strategic adviser in a large energy company. One of the aspects of the job that gives him most satisfaction is having healthy debate and helping others to see things differently. He told me how he had been in a meeting which his boss also attended and they had disagreed over a particular point. His boss called him in after the meeting and gave him a 30-minute "ear bashing", telling him that it was not acceptable to disagree with him publicly.
>
> I asked what this discussion had done to his motivation and how he would assess it on a scale of 1 to 10 (where 10 is high).

> "It's dropped to a 1," he said. "I'll now put all my energy into getting my MBA from INSEAD, and when I've done that, I'll leave."
>
> Sometimes your best option is to recognise which battles you will never win and step around them.

Clarify your personal goals

You may have found this chapter challenging. The questions are not meant to be easy, and you may have concluded that there are some major changes you want to make to realign with what's important for you.

Let's finish with rechecking the direction you are heading in. I have met many people who have not done this exercise and it can produce a few surprises. When I first did it, my life changed direction in several ways. I wrote down the responses to the questions and still have the piece of paper because it was so important to me. I'll share the detail of my responses later in the book.

Imagine yourself three years from now. (If that is too far, come back to one year.) Ask yourself these questions:

What do I want?

How will I know when I've achieved it?

What will I be doing then that I am not doing now?

Where and with whom will I be doing it?

How will it enhance my life?

How will I be feeling?

What are the five areas I need to work on in order to achieve this?

What are the first steps I need to take on the five areas?

When will I take them?

Again, I suggest sharing this with someone you trust. Once you describe to someone else the actions you plan to take, your commitment will increase and that person can support you and hold you accountable. Keep the plan visible and review it regularly. I update my five actions every year (on New Year's Day, along with other family members. We have great fun asking for an annual report on achievements and holding each other accountable!). I print it out and keep it on my desk as well as on my phone.

One final thought: it's up to you whether you take action from this chapter. You are your own stakeholder. Doing nothing is an option. Tell yourself it's been interesting (hopefully) and move on. If, however, anything in the chapter has caused you to experience what we might call an "itch", I suggest you scratch it. Ask yourself what you want to be able to say 10 years from now about how you dealt with your itch. I know I ignored several itches along my career and lost a lot of time and energy because of it.

If you believe we only get one go on this beautiful planet, how long are you prepared to wait for something to change?

Summary

If in this chapter you have found some meaningful answers to questions you hadn't considered before, you may have new insight into why your career mojo might not be running sweetly. I hope that feels good and your head is now full of thoughts about what you need to change.

Try not to allow yourself to be overwhelmed. This can feel like a massive challenge. Take a first step towards what you want and you may find, as I did, that events start to build on themselves, and before you know it you have built up great momentum towards your destination. I hope you enjoy the ride.

"The last of human freedoms – to choose one's attitude in any given set of circumstances, to choose one's own way."
Victor Frankl[22]

If I could wish for only one thing on your behalf from this book, it would be that it helps you to focus on what's important. Let's finish with this quote attributed to 85-year-old Kentucky resident Nadine Stair.[23]

If I had my life to live over, I'd dare to make more mistakes next time. I'd relax. I would limber up. I would be sillier than I have been this trip. I would take fewer things seriously. I would take more chances. I would climb more mountains and swim more rivers. I would eat more ice cream and less beans. I would have perhaps more actual troubles, but I'd have fewer imaginary ones.

You see, I'm one of those people who live sensibly and sanely hour after hour, day after day. Oh, I've had my moments, and if I had it to do over again, I'd have more of them. In fact, I'd try to have nothing else. Just moments, one after another, instead of living so many years ahead of each day. I've been one of those persons who never goes anywhere without a thermometer, a hot water bottle, a raincoat and a parachute. If I had to do it again, I would travel lighter than I have. If I had my life to live over, I would start barefoot earlier in the spring and stay that way late in the fall.

I would go to more dances, I would ride more merry-go-rounds. I would pick more daisies.

Questions

- What are you missing?

- What questions do you need to be asking yourself?

- What questions do others need to be asking?

- Why haven't you been asking these before now?

- What have you lost sight of?

Tool 2. Build more trust

"Trust is like the air we breathe. When it's there, no one notices. But when it's absent, everybody notices."

Warren Buffett

Of course I trust you Smithers, but next time we need toilet rolls please raise a purchase order for me to sign.

Introduction

Trust is on the slide, for all sorts of reasons. This has major ramifications in the workplace. In this chapter we'll look at why this is, consider the impact and then look at a tool to help you counteract this worrying trend.

Trust at work

Trust is a magic ingredient in the workplace. When you have high levels of trust you can collaborate, you can deal with change, you can build a truly high-performance team. It's essential if you're negotiating for a win/win outcome, where both parties can feel satisfied with the result. It can take years to build and seconds to destroy. "Trust arrives on foot but leaves on horseback," as the Dutch politician Johan Thorbecke once wrote. In today's global economy, success is driven by partnering, collaborating and sharing. Relationships are more critical than ever, and trying to do business without trust is like trying to build an office block on a sand dune.

Let's start by agreeing a definition of trust. I like Denise Rousseau's version:

Trust is "the intention to accept vulnerability based upon positive expectations of the intentions or behaviour of another".[24]

In an uncertain and volatile world, being able to rely on the positive intentions of others is critical.

Research tells us that there is a strong link between trust levels and employee engagement. Trust also impacts on productivity: researchers at the University of Sheffield found that high trust levels lead to productivity levels 5% above the average.[25] Sadly, the research also tells us that trust levels are on the slide. According to the PWC Annual Global CEO Survey 2017, 58% of CEOs are concerned that lack of trust will harm business growth, up from 37% four years ago.[26]

Why are trust levels so weak?

I once ran a Leadership workshop for senior managers in a major corporation in Europe. One of the topics we worked on was storytelling. We looked at some theory and a couple of examples on video, then got into groups to develop some of their own stories.

I told the group we would like to hear what they had come up with. I asked for a volunteer to start the ball rolling and vacated my seat in the middle of the room.

Nothing happened. The room fell totally silent and no one moved a muscle. Amazed, and perplexed, I quickly realised this was an important moment. I too sat there in silence. Thirty seconds in, I knew this was now a major test which I had to win. Twenty-five sets of eyes remained fixed on the floor, and still nothing. About two minutes of agony later, the boss stood up and gave his story. We gave some feedback and he sat down. "Who's next?" I said. Again, nothing. Eventually the second in command stood up and did his, and so it went on down the pecking order. The whole exercise took twice as long as it should have because of all the hanging around.

The next morning I felt I should explore this with the group. How come that happened? What were you all thinking? Fortunately, someone had the courage to give me an honest answer.

"I didn't want to tell my story because my boss is in the room and I didn't want to mess up in front of him."

This, of course, got us into a great discussion about trust and how being a hierarchical organisation for many years had built a low-trust culture which inhibited risk taking. From then on we were able to build a trusting dynamic in the room, which led to a very powerful (and emotional) experience for everyone. By letting go and being vulnerable, that person helped others to be vulnerable too, and that allowed us to build. It was a graphic demonstration of how debilitating low trust can be.

For a start, we humans are becoming less trusting. The Edelman Trust Barometer looks at responses from more than 30,000 people worldwide. The 2017 report concluded that trust in business, government, media and NGOs is "in crisis". It concluded:[27]

"With the fall of trust, the majority of respondents now lack full belief that the overall system is working for them. In this climate, people's societal and economic concerns, including globalization, the pace of innovation and eroding social values, turn into fears, spurring the rise of populist actions now playing out in several Western-style democracies."

Those of you educated in the school of "If you can't measure it, it's meaningless" management might appreciate a bit more data. The 2018 report showed no improvement:[28]

"Trust in UK business has fallen 3% to 43%, the lowest level since 2012. The most commonly cited barriers to rebuilding trust in business are as follows:

1. Top executives are overpaid relative to average workers (58%).

2. Businesses do not pay their fair share of tax (56%).

3. Businesses do not operate in a fair and transparent way (45%).

4. Corruption is commonly accepted (42%).

5. The average worker is mistreated or taken advantage of (42%).

A 2011 survey carried out by Maritz Research concluded that only 7% of employees strongly agreed that senior managers are consistent between their words and their actions. "Poor communication, lack of perceived caring, inconsistent behavior and perceptions of favoritism were cited as the largest contributors to the lack of trust in senior leaders."[29]

As we shall see later in the chapter, doing what you say you are going to do is a key component in building trust. We have all seen what faking it looks like: some politicians are particularly adept at it, and it really destroys our feeling of respect for them. Unfortunately, we get to see it all too often in the workplace. As author and London Business School professor Robert Goffee says:

"Nothing betrays the aspiring leader quite so much as the attempt to persuade others to do things that they would never do themselves."[30]

So what else is causing this low level of trust? One problem area is the prevalence of social media and our addiction to it. Its intrusion into our lives causes us to spend time communicating through our devices when we should be talking to each other. We've all seen hilarious (or is it pitiful?) examples of it: the two people sitting on the same sofa sending each other texts; the four people sitting together in a restaurant, each gazing at their device. We check our devices too often, we let them intrude on important conversations, we broadcast messages but fail to communicate. This is a widely acknowledged dysfunction in society, leading to a breakdown in human relationships, which itself breaks down levels of trust. It takes determined action to do anything about it.

Another source of damage to trust is job insecurity. This stems partly from the advance of technology. Artificial intelligence is upon us, and with companies such as Google, Tesla and Amazon investing millions in removing the human component from services, many job roles will simply cease to exist. The online solicitor, bank clerk, receptionist, doctor even. A major UK insurer, Prudential, has recently asked employees to volunteer for enhanced redundancy terms if they envisage their job could be automated within five years.

Even if our jobs aren't disappearing in the foreseeable future, we can also feel insecure from the regular restructuring that takes place. Researchers at the University of Sheffield have identified a clear link between reorganisation and low trust levels. Last year I carried out my own research project and asked several hundred employees about their job – many showed a high level of concern over job security. When you start spending extra energy protecting your job and proving your value, you reduce your willingness to collaborate and you are less likely to show vulnerability. This again is an important component of trust, as we'll see later.

Two other important factors that mitigate against high levels of trust are shortage of time and remote working. Employees are under increasing amounts of time pressure. As I said at the beginning of the book, the "more with less" mantra has been chanted incessantly for years now, and there simply is no slack in the system. When you don't have time to anticipate the next crisis before it hits you, you're less likely to invest time in exploring options with a colleague when a conflict arises. Instead you bash out your email response (probably it's overly direct and poorly worded), hit "Send" and move on. Damage done, and that person may want to get you back at some point.

Remote working, whether from home or from a different country (and time zone potentially), is also a major factor. Trust is built on relationships, and by definition if you rarely (or sometimes never) get to meet people in person, it is far harder to get to know them. When your communication is at best via a video call (in which, for some extraordinary reason, most people choose not to turn on the video camera) or at worst via email or some internal chat application, it is easy for it to be misinterpreted. If I misinterpret your communication, you may question my competence, it may produce conflict or chaos, and we are not going to trust each other as we did before.

Imagine this is an email I sent to you:

"I did not say my boss is a fool."

Pause for a moment and ask yourself what this sentence means. Now read it again, this time emphasising the word underlined.

"*I* did not say my boss is a fool." John did.

"I did not *say* my boss is a fool." I wrote that he is.

"I did not say *my* boss is a fool." I said yours is.

"I did not say my boss is a *fool*." I said she is a complete blithering idiot.

Without tone or body language, email is a highly dangerous tool and the source of much workplace damage. If in doubt, pick up the phone or go to see the person if you can.

In conclusion, we see trust levels breaking down in society as a whole. We compound the problem with our behaviours, and because we feel less secure in our jobs, we feel less inclined to open up with other people.

What's the impact?

If we do not trust someone, we feel threatened. Our brains switch into defensive mode and we seek to protect ourselves. In one way or another we will display Fight, Flight or Freeze responses. Attack the other person (not physically, one would hope), avoid them or do nothing. Hardly the ingredients for a collaborative and high-performing team.

We spend time defending ourselves, attempting to look good at every opportunity and covering our backs with an auditable trail of email and documentation just in case anyone should point the finger at us. Hugely wasting our own and others' time in the process. As Stephen MR Covey puts it, "As trust goes down, speed goes down and costs go up."[31]

This type of behaviour can manifest itself in all sorts of ways. One of them I encounter a lot is in the way people communicate on a conference call or in a meeting. Imagine you are leading the discussion, trying to get others to buy in to a new working practice you are leading. If you do not trust people in the room, you may fear their responses. Some people try to counteract that by minimising others' opportunity to respond. They do all the talking, try not to allow any silence, and do what they can to keep questions to the end. A one-way transmission, followed by a swift exit from the room. Instead of encouraging a dialogue and thus understanding, recognising and respecting others' views, they force the message down the audience's throats. Far from influencing, they may have alienated. Relationships are now weaker than they were before.

Weak and non-trusting relationships can also waste huge amounts of time. If I am your boss and I don't trust you, chances are I don't delegate as much as I should (thus causing you not to learn and grow, and causing me to do the wrong job). You will remain a Child in this relationship and I will be your Parent (a controlling one at that, checking up on you and effectively policing the work you do). I expand more on Parent–Child relationships in the section on transactional analysis in Tool 4.

This micromanaging style is all too prevalent, in my experience. Over the years I have been informally researching what percentage of teams are made up of people who come to work with a predominantly Child Ego state. Most people assess it between 20% and 30%. This is such a missed opportunity. If only these Parents, who prefer to manage using a Directive style, could learn to engage as Adults with their team (by asking more questions, opening themselves up, exploring more options than the ones they had in mind), the Children in the organisation could once more step up, take on more responsibility and start to thrive again as Adults.

Poor trust levels damage productivity, result in weak decision making and debate, and cause others not to develop and achieve their potential. It damages morale and is a major inhibitor of career mojo.

How to develop trust

It's hard not to agree that having high levels of trust at work is a good thing. How, then, can we go about building it?

Trust is something we have to work towards. Here is a model you can use to enable you to do that in a conscious way.

The CORE model of trust

In order for you to trust me, I need to build up four trust elements in your mind (CORE):

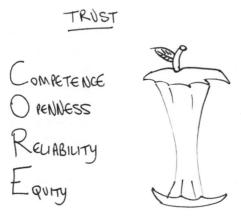

Let's examine each one.

Competence. I need to demonstrate competence as quickly as possible. You need to see me as the right person to talk to. I need to show you I know my stuff, have done my preparation and maybe have done this before. If you're negotiating with me, it helps if you know that I can make decisions and have authority to do a deal with you.

> *Simple example:* I once worked as a supervisor in a warehouse. We hired a temporary forklift truck driver. He was quite young but was keen and he told us he had driven forklifts before and had a licence to prove it. The first day he jumped onto the forklift it had been raining and the warehouse floor was wet. He drove too fast and within minutes had smacked into the side of a lorry. He was on floor-sweeping duty until I had a chance to supervise and coach him in using this particular type of vehicle. Trust was certainly an issue based on that event.

Openness. If you are to trust me, I need to be open with you. Closed behaviour will cause you not to trust me. If I whisper to a colleague while you're talking, or make secretive notes, you might not trust me. If I show no reaction when you make a concession or do something helpful, you might not trust me. Poker players with poker faces might win games but they are probably not good at getting others to trust them. If I don't say much, or avoid your questions, you might not trust me. If I refuse to share information or keep things from you, it can damage trust. The wine waiter who tries to sell you a wine without you seeing the price might be someone you don't trust.

Reliability. Doing what you say you are going to do. Walking the talk. Being consistent and predictable. These are all things that will build trust. The train which always leaves on time. The driver who always shows up 10 minutes early to collect you just in case. The boss who says she'll get you a decision on your pay rise by the end of the week and makes a point of doing so. This trust component is often the most fragile. You only have to let someone down once and you can severely damage a relationship. Do it twice and you can do it for life.

Equity. This means fairness. Our relationship has to be fair if you are going to trust me. It has to be a two-way street. I give you something, you give me something back. If I do all the giving and you do all the taking, it will erode trust. So when you offer to be helpful in some way, I will try to find a way to be helpful back.

> A: *"Yes, I think I can move my meeting back so we can meet up on Friday."*

> B: *"Excellent, would it help if I came over to your place?"*

Using the CORE model really works, and it can not only help build relationships and trust, it will also help you make negotiation less competitive and stressful.

I once met someone on one of my training programmes who was involved in leading a major upcoming training project for his employer. We got talking and I soon realised that there was potential for my training company to be involved, and that if successful it would be one of our biggest ever consultancy projects. The sums involved would normally have meant that his company would go out to tender for the contract.

I actively used the CORE approach to build a trusting relationship with Derek. This involved making an opportunity to have dinner with him on a couple of occasions while travelling, and having lunch at his house a couple of times as well. (There is nothing quite like sharing a meal and a glass of wine to build trust, in my experience.) During this time I had plenty of opportunity to establish Competence, create Openness, demonstrate Reliability and suggest creative ways of making this a great two-way relationship (Equity), without ever actually pitching anything to him. When it came to awarding the contract, Derek rang me one Friday afternoon, said he'd like to go ahead at the consultancy rates I had suggested, and could I start next month? No formal tender process or pitching against the competition. Derek trusted me, and for him that was enough.

Using the CORE model

There may be some critical relationships where you need to establish (or maybe re-establish) trust. If you don't have a trusting relationship with your boss, might I suggest that this should be your number one priority to fix? The challenge is to plan how you can use CORE to support your relationship. How quickly can you prove Competence? Is there information you can share to demonstrate that you are the right person to talk to? How do you establish your credentials?

What can you do to be Open with the other person? Can you give away some information without damaging your position? Maybe you can be open with an emotion, for instance. "We're a little anxious as we're not quite sure what this means." "I'm a bit confused as I've not come across this before." Often when you open up in this way, the other person will reciprocate and you can then build on this by being open on something more important, and again they may reciprocate. Gradually the relationship becomes less guarded and you move towards a much honest and meaningful dialogue.

You can plan your Reliability. Only commit to something you can guarantee you can deliver on. It doesn't have to be huge: "I'll send you the agenda tomorrow morning." Make sure you do, and in a subtle way the other person trusts you that little bit more. Do it regularly and the impression that you are an honourable and trustworthy person will build.

Finally, be aware of the need for Equity. Make an effort to give back whenever you can. Be the first to make a move: the chances are the other party will give you something back when you do. "Reciprocity", as this might be called, is well proven as a tool for influence. Dr Robert Cialdini goes into this in detail in his book *Influence: the psychology of persuasion*.[32] His research shows that when using this Principle of Reciprocity, the key is to be the first to give, and to make the gift personalised and unexpected. He gives an excellent example of how waiters who give a mint to the customer when they present the bill see a 3% increase in tips, rising to 14% when they give two mints and rising to 23% if they give one mint, walk away and then turn back, saying, "For you nice people, here's an extra mint." Make it personalised for extra impact.

I just want to add one more thing on the subject of openness. As we work towards high levels of trust, we don't want to be open about everything. As Robert Goffee put it: "We want to get close, but not too close."[33]

So we need to think about what we can disclose that will move towards increased openness while at the same time not undermining our credibility. You might win Openness points for saying "I have no idea how that happened" while losing points on the Competence scale, as I once did as head waiter after I had showered the guest, his wife and the occupants of the next table in his own very expensive champagne.

Openness requires taking a degree of risk. What will happen if we are open but the other party does not reciprocate? We have shown our hand, but they haven't. This can happen, and so risk taking is involved. Win/win always requires a degree of courage. It's called leadership.

Ian Walker is a director in a major tech company. He gave me this nice example:

"I used to have a boss who often welled up with tears when he talked about members of his team and his pride in their achievements: it was immensely powerful. He did it in all-hands meetings with hundreds of people as well as in much smaller team meetings – it was authentic and consistent and reflected his honest sense of being moved.

"Equally, there was a European president of a former company where I worked who spoke enthusiastically about topics about which he was passionate, but struggled when asked questions about things which he felt were less important to the success of the business. He tried to fake it, but to everyone listening, it was like night and day."

I finish this chapter with an example of Openness I witnessed. In one moment someone was able to communicate in a way that transformed the levels of trust in his management team and led to a paradigm shift in his business's performance.

I was facilitating a team workshop for a leading retailer in the UK called Peter Jones, part of the John Lewis chain of stores. The flagship store in Kensington, London had just had a multi-million refit and the whole management team was invited to an offsite event designed to build relationships and trust and prepare for the challenges of reopening the store and meeting stretching new targets.

I put together a team of facilitators and we arranged an event in which the team was required to write and record an original music album in just two days, and to use it to raise money for charity. When we issued the brief, 30 managers gazed back at us in a mixture of horror, amazement and incredulity. Clearly thinking we

> were mad, they set about the task. Needless to say, we got our five-track album, which we listened to at the end of the event. They raised thousands of pounds for a charity for disabled children and by the end emotions were running high.
>
> I did my closing piece, congratulating them on the achievement and noting what behaviours had led to their success. I then handed over for a few final words from the managing director, Paul Hunt. He intended to tell them what the new targets were and remind them of the importance of success when they got back to work. The emotion of the moment got to him, however, and all he managed to say was "I'm ... so ... proud" before the tears started to quietly roll down his cheeks. He stood there crying, in what was one of the most powerful speeches I have ever seen. Needless to say, everyone else was soon crying and hugging, too. His openness and vulnerability led to the same from everyone else and the team went back to work with trusting relationships like never before. They went on to smash every one of the performance targets they had been set and they still talk about the event years later.

Developing trusting relationships with your colleagues and stakeholders is like putting top-quality oil in your mojo engine. If people trust you, things will run so much more smoothly. You can afford the occasional cockup if people trust you, because we're all human. Mess up too often and it's a different story, of course. But for now, have a think about how trusting you are of others and where you need to focus some more effort. We'll come back to Trust later in Tool 5, when we talk about Negotiation, as there too it is the oil between the wheels and can transform the deals you do.

Summary

Using the CORE model, you can plan how to build trust with the key people in your network. Investing time in this (and unfortunately that is easier said than done, as I am all too aware) will pay off because you will be able to build a meaningful and more open relationship with these people and therefore save a lot of time in not having to play games with each other. You will find it makes relationships more enjoyable and far less stressful. A real boost to your career mojo if ever there was one.

Questions

- How well do you trust the key people in your workplace?

- How well do you think they trust you?

- How can you use CORE to build trust in the most important relationships?

- Where can you be more vulnerable?

- What can you disclose without damaging credibility?

Make some notes on actions you need to take if you recognise that building Trust with some key people in your network is worth more of your time.

Tool 3. Get out of the playground

"How is it that there can be so many sources of power, yet so many feelings of powerlessness?"

Gareth Morgan

Sir, in the light of this month's excellent sales we wondered if we might be allowed out to play?

Introduction

There are times when your interactions with other people do not go as well as you'd like. That hurried phone conversation with your boss that leaves you wanting to kick the cat. That meeting you walk out of where everyone appeared to agree with the new policy but secretly most of you thought it an act of madness. The conversation over dinner when your partner suggested having her mum stay for Christmas and you reacted badly, leading to eating the rest of the meal in silence. That type of interaction. All too frequent?

There's a way of avoiding them and this chapter is going to show you how.

Analysing your transactions

Let me introduce you to a favourite model which will give us a language to help us analyse the transactions you have with others. Funnily enough, it's called transactional analysis. This model, which has its roots in the work of Sigmund Freud, was developed by American psychiatrist Dr Eric Berne in the 1950s. If you want to go into more detail, read Berne's *Games people play*[34] and Thomas Harris's *I'm OK, you're OK*.[35]

Let me give a brief overview, just to introduce the language so that we can do some of our own analysis.

At any one moment in time you and I have an ego state: a set of thoughts, feelings and behaviours which creates a personality style. We can be either a Parent (P), Adult (A) or Child (C).

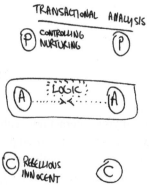

There are two styles of Parent: Controlling and Nurturing. You're familiar with both, and use them regularly:

"Ring me when you get there, and make sure you're back before midnight." Controlling.

"Have a lovely time, and say hi to Joe's mum for me." Nurturing. Nurturing Parents allow the Child to play and learn and set fewer rules for them.

Adult state is the means by which we regulate our Parent and Child states. It is a state in which we are most likely to be able to remain objective. When two Adults are "transacting", the exchange will have more logic and less emotion than in the other two states. It's the "grown-up" version of ourselves in which we are most comfortable, and we will display reasonable and assertive behaviour in this state. For many, it is our "ideal self".

There are two styles of Child: Rebellious or Innocent. Rebellious are the ones with an agenda, and are generally more trouble to deal with. They come in noisy and silent varieties: the noisy ones you deal with by telling them to leave the table and go to their room; the silent ones are harder to spot sometimes – they're the ones with long faces who won't engage unless you make them. You know the sort.

Innocent Children are far more fun to be with, and they like to learn through play and just being children. They have no agenda and are happy to be guided on what to do and what not to do.

A time and place for all ego states

All three ego states have a role to play in the workplace. You flip in and out of them from minute to minute, and much of the time this is fine. We need some Parent in the room when a decision is required and we don't have much time. A Parent is useful for explaining to us how the new security system is going to work. We may need a Parent to chair the disciplinary meeting for the employee who broke the security protocols.

Adult-to-Adult transactions are great where we want to discuss things freely: where there is no right or wrong and we want to involve people on an equal power footing. A great way to hold a coaching conversation. Great for team problem solving.

Child ego state has its place, too: accessing Child state unlocks creativity, intuition, spontaneous drive and fun. It is often overlooked and sometimes frowned upon, which I think is a shame. This can lead to loss of curiosity, the ability to dream, naivety, innocence, and deep and pure emotions. As the writer Alan Bennett once said: "Were we closer to the grass as children, or is the grass emptier now?"

Analysing transactions

Think of a recent transaction you had with someone and try to work out what the ego states were (both yours and the other party's). How was the other person's ego state influencing yours, and vice versa?

Here's a crucial point: this is a bit of a "which came first, the chicken or the egg?" question. Was their ego state a response to yours, or was it the other way round? If I become your Parent, it is very hard for you not to become my Child.

Where did it all go wrong?

Like many things in life, when you get the timing wrong it can lead to problems. Workplace dysfunctionality can come about when we get crossed wires, which we don't want, or where the ego state is wrong for the situation.

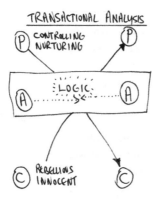

TRANSACTIONAL ANALYSIS

P CONTROLLING NURTURING

P

LOGIC

A

A

C REBELLIOUS INNOCENT

C

 Let's analyse a personal crossed-wire situation. Put your hand over the right side of the page to see whether you analyse the ego states involved in the same way as I do.

This happened more than 30 years ago, but I remember it as if it were yesterday. It was when I was a regional manager for a chain of eight restaurants. It was 9pm Christmas Eve and my wife and I had just sat down for a special meal she'd spent hours preparing. The fire was crackling in the hearth and the carols were playing in the background.

The phone rang. It was the manager from my biggest restaurant in outer London.

"Mr Brown, it's Chris here from the Red Lion." (He was shouting down the phone to make himself heard above the din of drinkers in his no doubt jam-packed bar.)

"Hello Chris. What a surprise to hear from you."	BARELY SUPRESSED DISGRUNTLED PARENT
"Sorry to interrupt your evening, Mr Brown, but I had to ring you. You see, we have run out of mince pies, and the punters are going crazy."	INNOCENT CHILD

> "I'm sorry to hear that, Chris. And what precisely are you expecting me to do about it?"   PARENT
>
> "I don't know really, I suppose I'm just wondering whether you've got any ideas."   INNOCENT CHILD
>
> "Yes, I do have an idea actually. Get your arse round to the corner shop, buy some effing mincemeat and tell your chef to make some. Good night."   CONTROLLING PARENT
>
> I'm not proud of it. Not good. Needless to say, this ruined my Christmas as I spent the next three days waiting for another call from Chris, this time to report running out of turkeys or something. Had I created a Rebellious Child who was going to get revenge by giving me more problems, or was he going to report me to senior management for failing to support him in his hour of need? Either way, I was now the Child in this relationship. Chris and I never really fixed this crossed-wire relationship, to my eternal shame.

How many Children in your team?

A question I often ask on my courses is what percentage of people in the workplace have an ongoing ego state that is Child. Some people are so used to being handled by a Parent that they give up trying to do Adult, as they find it too exhausting and dispiriting. Far easier just to sit back, relax and wait to be told what to do. This in turn causes the Parent to have to do even more Parent, and leads to micromanagement by the Parent and disengagement by the Child.

What's your answer to that question? What's the percentage?

Over the years the answer has averaged between 20% and 30%. This seems to me to be such a wasted opportunity. If these people could regain their Adult ego state when they need it, they might be capable of so much more and undoubtedly they'd find more satisfaction and happiness while at work.

What brings out the Child in you?

If you recognise that your Child comes out to play at work when perhaps it should not, it's worth working out what triggers it. Might it be:

- Someone who by virtue of their seniority, expertise, experience, class just somehow makes you feel inferior? Maybe not deliberately perhaps, but somehow they just do?

- Certain situations in which you do not feel qualified to be at the table?

- Not being in control in some way: needing more time to prepare, needing more information?

- Not agreeing with something and not feeling that you can voice it – maybe because the people in head office issued it and others around you believe that what head office says is truth and cannot be debated?

- Feeling weaker because of where you work (from home, in another time zone, not on the same continent as HQ)?

- Feeling vulnerable because of language or not understanding the jargon?

- Being new to the role? (Note: I have met so many people who carry the mental label "I'm new around here" for far too long – in some cases for more than a year.)

It's a choice

Your ego state is a choice you make. You can choose to respond to others in a Child way: no one can force you. It's a decision you make in the millisecond you have before you respond to that trigger, be it an annoying email or a rude comment made in a meeting.

Part of the answer here is to slow down your response: pause before responding. This gives your brain a chance to recover from what is sometimes called "The Amygdala Hijack" and to remember that there is more than one response available to you.

These choices can make a huge difference to your well-being and even your health.

A friend of mine, Alastair Backus, is a physiotherapist in a private clinic in Plymouth. He spends his life helping people overcome injuries. In his line of work, they characterise people, maybe a little harshly, into "copers" and "non-copers". Their path to recovery can be very different.

"You can see two people with similar injuries, similar age and situation, who will have a vastly different path to recovery. Person A with mechanical back pain will see it as her responsibility to get fit again and will see me as a resource to facilitate that. Person B thinks I am some sort of magician who is going to make her symptoms disappear and takes a passive role in the recovery path. She will tell me how she is never going to be able to play tennis again and how hard life is going to be from here on. The mental attitude that people bring is in many ways far more important than the injury itself. Certainly, for mechanical low back pain one of the biggest predictors of a patient's outcome is what their perceived outcome is at the start."

I think of Person B here as having a victim mentality, and I see it all too often. Are you condemned to these dysfunctional relationships for life, or can you actually do something about it? Of course, you can do something about it, and you have already made a start by buying this book and making the time to read it. You're already halfway there!

How to get out of the playground

And so to the crux of it. If you recognise where your Child ego state is getting in the way of a fruitful relationship, and you have identified some triggers, we now just need to know how to adapt our behaviour so we can get out of the playground.

The great news here is that while you can't change the other person (and neither should you try to), you can change their response to you. To do that you have to change your behaviour – and you are totally in control of that decision. Ponder that for a while if you like, as it is important.

That means you need to make the first move. Don't wait for things to evolve in your favour, because they probably won't. Be proactive, and be ready to take the risk of making the first move. You will be amazed at how good that feels, and what difference it can make.

What is that first move? It is to apply an Adult mindset. Put on an Adult hat. If it helps, become the person you most admire for their Adult attitudes – mentally become them for this transaction. Then repeat.

With a bit of luck, the other person will meet you as Adult, even if they normally display Parent towards you. (Remember the chicken and egg: maybe they were your Parent because you went first as Child?)

One of my least successful relationships at work was with my boss when I worked in the restaurant business (a rich seam, I am finding, for personal misery anecdotes). From the off he treated me as Parent, and I never managed to break the mould. I remember one transaction in particular, probably because it was so extreme.

I was driving to Swansea to "inspect" (a word used a lot in this particular business) my grottiest restaurant. Boss from Hell (BFH) paged me (this was pre mobile phones) so I had to come off the motorway and find a functioning phone box (it took me half an hour). I rang him, heart pumping, as surely this was an emergency?

BFH: "Mr Brown [he liked to use surnames – a way of keeping people at arm's length, I guess]. What took you so long?"

Me: "Sorry Martin, I couldn't find a phone box."

BFH: "Excuses, excuses. Pull the other leg. Now, Mr Brown. I came into the office this morning and walked past the front door of your restaurant downstairs. There was an empty cigarette packet right in front of the main entrance. Now you get back here and see that fat lazy cow of a manager. Tell her from me that the next time I have to walk past a cigarette packet in front of one of my restaurants she will get fired."

Me: (Gulp) "I'm in Bristol now, so can't see her till this evening. I'll ring her now and get it removed."

BFH: "You make sure you do. Have a nice day."

What I should have done, but lacked maybe the skills and the mental willingness (perhaps because I was still carrying the "I'm new around here" label), was what one of my more experienced regional manager colleagues used to do, which was to stand up to Martin. As with all bullies, the best thing you can do is up your energy level and draw a line in the sand. Peter would have had no qualms in telling Boss from Hell that an occasional erroneous cigarette packet is not grounds for dismissal, and that as he was the person who walked past it, a better option might have been for him to have given the manageress feedback. In other words, Peter would meet BFH with some Parental style and then slip into

> Adult dialogue.
> All easier said than done in the heat of the moment, or when the "amygdala hijack" kicks in. No one is saying this is easy. 🍿

You might want to think through how your amended transaction is going to sound. Visualise it. Role play it with a friend even.

"Boss, I was hoping we could meet up so we could discuss an idea I have" becomes:

"John, I have a proposal I think you'd want to see, can we meet at 2 for 10 minutes to go through it?"

If your Child is triggered, for instance, when making a presentation and realising there are experts in the room, the best way to defuse them is to acknowledge them as experts. Then they don't have to prove it by asking you nasty questions. Try inserting this type of language into the opening of your next presentation: "I know there is a lot of experience and expertise in the room today, and I really want to make sure we use that, so please feel free to add in where relevant as I go through the presentation." Now that they feel acknowledged, they are on your side. You have made yourself bulletproof.

Similarly, a great way to get Parents who are doing Parent as a power statement to become Adult is to acknowledge them. It's a bit like a little dog meeting a big dog: one way they handle that is to roll over and effectively say with their body language "You're a big dog. Wow, look at your big teeth and that massive tail!" Big Dog feels acknowledged and can now be OK to be Adult with Little Dog.

This can be done with language, quite subtly. "Clearly this is your decision, but here are the two options I'd recommend." Or, "I know you're busy: when would work best for you?"

For more on this topic of dealing with power, Roger Fisher's book *Beyond reason*[36] is well worth a read. It explains how to deal with the five "core concerns" of individuals: appreciation, affiliation, autonomy, status and role. Using his suggestions will create many options for generating an Adult response in others.

Summary

Many of your unsatisfactory transactions can probably be characterised as some form of "crossed wire" (a Parent–Child transaction where you are Child and wish you could get to Adult, but can't). They will often cause you stress, dissatisfaction and even misery, and no doubt undermine your self-confidence and lead to career mojo loss.

You *can* fix this! It takes a bit of courage and some thinking through, but you can do it. When you do, it has the power to transform a relationship for the better.

I urge you not to delay, and to make the first move. The worst thing that can happen is it makes no difference. But even so, you will know you tried and can therefore feel better about yourself.

Questions

- Where can you apply the CORE model?

- Where will you get most benefit if it works?

- How can you change your approach to help others to move from Child state?

- How else can you generate a more Adult environment in your team?

Make some notes on actions you can take to get started.

Tool 4. Invest in relationships

"In the normal course of events, we do not listen to discover what the other person's reality is. We only listen to evaluate the rightness or wrongness of the other person's reality compared to our own."

Stewart Emery

Well boss perhaps we could do
My performance review now?

Introduction

You have too much to do and not enough time to do it. One of the first things to suffer when this is the case is the time you invest in building relationships. Both at work and outside, there are some people who are key players in your world, and having an open, trusting and collaborative relationship with these people is an essential component in a well-functioning career mojo.

There's hard evidence to back this up. Research of more than 30,000 executives in the US and Canada by Leadership IQ showed that "most people spend only half the time they should be spending with their boss. People who do spend an optimal number of hours interacting with their direct leader (six hours per week) are 29% more inspired, 30% more engaged, 16% more innovative and 15% more intrinsically motivated than those who spend only one hour per week".[37]

You already knew that, of course. This chapter more than anything is a wake-up call to ring fence more time to invest in building (or more likely rebuilding) those key relationships, along with one or two tools to help you do so.

Assess yourself

Relationships aren't given to you – they have to be earned. I always say you get the relationship you deserve: if your relationship with your boss is malfunctioning and you haven't done anything about it, arguably you have only yourself to blame. Let's say she has a habit of cancelling your one-to-one meetings at the last minute and you let it really annoy you because it makes you feel undervalued. If you don't give her some feedback about this, you will continue to feel bad about it, and the chances are it will keep on happening. Whose fault is that?

Some relationships are more important than others. We'll use a tool later in the chapter to help you assess which ones are most worth investing in. The really important ones (your boss, your project sponsor, your top client maybe) have to be based on mutual understanding of what is important, some agreed goals, agreed ways of working and so on. Otherwise you run the risk of being what one of my clients the other day described as "a busy fool". Without knowing what is important, you run a life of what I call "spray and pray": rushing around doing lots of activity in the hope that some of it will be seen as useful and relevant. A recipe for burnout and mojo loss.

Is it time for you to start making more time for relationships? Have you lost sight of how sterile your relationships are becoming? Have we all forgotten the basic skills of being human with each other?

Making time for it

The biggest problem with all of this is the usual enemy – time. "I'm too busy fighting fires to do this" is the oft-heard response to this suggestion. The point being, of course, that if you had better relationships you might not have so many fires to put out. If you think this is important, you may need to plan the time for it and ring fence it (using the usual techniques: book a meeting with yourself, schedule meetings with these people in which the agenda is to look at how you can work more effectively together). If it's important enough, you won't let the time stealers impinge on it.

What does good look like?

Good relationships are built by deploying emotional intelligence. In these relationships, people are able to open up with each other and let their humanity out. They genuinely care about the other person, and are honest, vulnerable and sincere towards them. They can see the other person's perspective, and even if they don't agree with it, they can understand it and empathise with it. Conflict levels are low because there is a high level of mutual respect. Both parties are working towards the same thing and collaborating on how to do so.

One way of assessing your relationship is to examine the levels of communication you have with this person.

Level 1: easy things – what you did at the weekend, latest politics, holidays, sport.

Level 2: more personal things – fears for your child's schooling, your passion for your hobby, some family news that makes you proud.

Level 3: deeply held important things – your aspirations, values, purpose, beliefs.

I have a Level 3 relationship with my business partner, Spencer Holmes. He and I co-founded How NOT 2 videos four years ago and have spent much time collaborating in the training room. Our level of mutual respect is high, based on having spent so much time together (including on a series of long-haul flights during a world tour) and it is fair to say we are able to talk about pretty much anything. We give each other regular and often challenging feedback, and spend time with each other talking about non-work-related things. I well remember a conversation following a service we attended at Westminster Abbey in which we talked about the contribution we wanted to make to society through charitable work and other means. Not often one finds oneself able to freely talk about such things.

The opposite, an example of a weak relationship, was when I was heading a marketing function reporting to the CEO. Jerry was a very busy man and I found it hard to get time with him. When we did meet it was to review progress against my to-do-list and we never really got round to exploring the important stuff, such as what our strategy was. As a result, I found myself in "spray and pray" mode, trying out lots of initiatives which rarely hit the spot as far as Jerry was concerned. We had regular misunderstandings, both of us avoided conflict most of the time, and I found myself having to be a mind reader (which I proved not to be very good at). Fortunately, this high-stress situation was resolved when I renegotiated my role (a crucial conversation which for once I got right) and found myself fruitfully deployed at last as a training consultant (and with a new boss, to our mutual relief).

99

Getting closer to your boss

I'd be surprised if your boss isn't featuring in your thinking as you go through this chapter. Even if it is a functional relationship, it may be capable of working even better. Here are some suggestions on how you might go about achieving that.

The most important thing is to ensure you exercise your right to a regular, constructive one-to-one meeting with your boss. Ideally once per month. Planned well in advance. (You could even schedule them for the whole year – these are important meetings, so why not get them in the schedule before others do?) Allow one hour. Consider location: maybe not across the desk from each other in the boss's office?

Note: if the only time you get with your boss for anything approaching a full one-to-one discussion is at the annual review (and I know this does happen), you have only yourself to blame. Assert your right to have these meetings, as it is in both your interests that you understand each other and are clear about what is important.

Plan the agenda and send it in advance. This shows you value the meeting and are being proactive. If your boss is an Introvert, they will appreciate having time to consider it in advance of the meeting, and you'll have shown respect. If you show someone respect, you usually get respect back.

Don't fill all the time with reviewing your progress against the previous to-do list. You can do that with a spreadsheet and send it before or after the meeting. Instead use it to cover much more important questions, such as:

- What are your current priorities? What's on your mind?
- What are your objectives and how can I best support them? How does what I do fit into the bigger picture?
- What would you like me to do more of and less of?
- How else could I increase my contribution to our success?
- What feedback do you have for me?
- How can you support my personal growth?
- What contingencies should we be planning for?
- What do you know that I should be aware of?

As you get into this, you may be able to venture into a Level 3 discussion of your personal values and hopes and aspirations.

You should walk away from these discussions with a clear understanding of what is important and how you can add value to your contribution. This allows you to prioritise, push back on non-important requests and reduce your "busy fool" efforts. Good news for you and for your boss, surely?

Know yourself

A great way to build relationships between people is to share information about personality types. There is no shortage of profiling tools available but I wanted to focus briefly on one of them. All are designed with two basic aims:

- To help people understand themselves better.

- To help them use this understanding to build better relationships with others.

I want to talk about the world's most widely used personality profiling tool, the Myers-Briggs® Type Indicator (MBTI®). This looks at four aspects of your personality and identifies your preference on each of four spectrums:

- Extraversion *v* Introversion. Where you get your energy.
- Sensing *v* Intuition. The type of information you pay attention to.
- Thinking *v* Feeling. How you prefer to make decisions.
- Judging *v* Perceiving. How you prefer to structure your life.

In the table below, you can see very high-level descriptions of the eight preferences. You will probably find yourself saying that you do bits of both and often it depends on the situation. Everyone is capable of inhabiting all of the boxes in the table – the question is, given a choice, which of those boxes would you prefer to inhabit?

Preferences

Extraversion	Introversion
Variety, action, interaction, discussing ideas, learn by talking and doing. Love interruptions.	Quiet for concentration, focus on project or task, develop ideas internally, learn by reading and reflecting. Hate interruptions.
Sensing	**iNtuition**
Immediate issues, realistic, practical, collect facts, use experience. See gaps, mistakes, detail.	Inspiration, love new problems, big picture, love change and new ways of doing things. See implications and patterns.
Thinking	**Feeling**
Focus on tasks, logic, analysis. Firm minded. Consistent.	Use values to decide. Empathetic, harmonious. Prefer consensus.
Judging	**Perceiving**
Plan. List making. Closure. On time.	Flexible. Open ended. Spontaneous.

If you have never done this profile before, might I suggest you complete it? It's hard to get through life without bumping into the MBTI® assessment, and once you know your preference, it is the basis of a really constructive conversation with someone else about this. I often ask people what their four-letter Myers-Briggs® profile is, particularly if they are a prospective client. You might say I would do that, wouldn't I, as I'm in the learning and development business. The thing is, if you ask this question, people often know their profile and will therefore get why you are asking. And if not, you might be able to persuade them to complete the profile.

Because you will both benefit. Let's take me as an example. I'm an ENFP (Extraversion, Intuition, Feeling and Perceiving preferences). I get energy from being with people, I shy away from detail, I make decisions empathetically and not always logically, and I prefer to improvise my way through life: plans are for dummies.

I meet a lot of ISTJs in my line of work (it's a classic profile for engineers, for instance). These people have 100% opposite preferences to mine. I am like an alien being to them. They prefer peace and quiet and minimal interaction with others, they enjoy detail, make logical and tough-minded decisions, and they *love* a plan.

No good or bad here, folks, just *different*.

Armed with my self-knowledge I can use it to help me build a better relationship with an ISTJ. I might correspond more via email, consciously reduce my energy a bit, think of the detailed questions an ISTJ might have, not get too hung up on tricky decisions, and make an attempt at a plan to assure the ISTJ that everything is in place to progress in an orderly fashion.

That's not me manipulating the ISTJ, it is me using self-awareness and adapting to the situation – basically using some emotional intelligence to connect more effectively with a person whose mindset is very different to mine.

You just might find that you can transform some of your key relationships simply by adapting your mindset towards someone with a different profile to yours. I have often said that it should be mandatory for both parties to complete the MBTI® profile before they let you get married. It should also be on the school curriculum for 16 year olds before they lock down on higher-level studies and start contemplating careers.

> The most miserable year of my life was when I was a regional manager in the restaurant business. The restaurants were part of a national chain, so everything about the operation had to support the brand, from the way a turkey was displayed on the carvery to the way employees answered the phone. My life was basically that of a policeman, ensuring that the restaurants complied in every respect with what was written in the brand policy manual. It was a lonely, introverted job (I drove 56,000 miles that year), requiring total attention to detail, tough-minded hiring and firing decisions almost every day, and complete adherence to a structure. An ISTJ job, and I'm an ENFP. It was like writing with my wrong hand for a year. I've never been so tired, stressed or unhappy. Had I known my MBTI® profile then, I would have avoided the job like the plague. Help your children to avoid the same trap – get them to do the MBTI® assessment as soon as they can (mid-teens onwards).

If you want to complete the profile, you can do it online or through a licensed MBTI® practitioner. I happen to offer Myers-Briggs® coaching and you can book a session through my website https://reallearningforachange.com/coaching/. Or contact OPP in the UK (www.opp.com/en/tools) or CPP in the US (www.cpp.com) for details of the global network of practitioners who can help you both to understand your profile and explore how to use this in your interactions with others, your career planning, etc.

Otto Kroeger's book *Type talk at work* is also an excellent read and will help you to make an intelligent guess at your profile without having to complete a questionnaire.[38]

There is great value to be had in exploring with key players in your network questions related to their preferences. Such things as:

- How much detail do we need for this?
- Do we need someone to help us with the detail (or to see and articulate the bigger picture)?
- Do we need a plan? How much should we plan?
- How shall we communicate? What works best for us?

Get yourself some decent objectives

One sign of relationship dysfunction is when people are working towards objectives that don't work as well as they should. Or even worse, when they don't have any written objectives (not as rare as you might think).

The idea behind setting annual objectives is to produce clarity over what is required and to give the individual something motivational to work towards. If they are set well, they can act as a real motivator and make a real difference to an individual's performance. (This is how athletes operate and how Roger Bannister first got round to running a mile in under four minutes.)

Set badly, they make little difference, are quickly forgotten and become the source of mutual embarrassment when they reappear at the next annual review and are disregarded, fudged or used as a stick with which to hit the individual.

If you have a good conversation around this with your boss, you have the basis of a good working contract for the next 12 months. Here are my suggestions for how to go about this.

1. Recognise the difference between a goal, a target and an objective. Well-formed objectives are initiatives you will undertake that will contribute to the achievement of the objectives your boss is working towards. Goals set out what you are seeking to accomplish. Targets are measures of success.

   Example

   Goal: achieve lowest operating costs in the business by year end.

   Target: operating costs reduced by 5% year on year by December 2019.

   Objective: implement three initiatives to reduce operating costs in the warehouse by June 2019.

2. Be proactive. Try to avoid being on the receiving end of a set of metrics cascaded down from on high and more than likely not initiatives but rather targets. Get there first: propose your objectives at a timely discussion with your boss, before the corporate stuff lands. By all means keep their targets to hand as well, of course, but the motivational stuff will be the key initiatives you agree between you as being most relevant and meaningful for the coming year.

3. Don't set more than five objectives. Cognitive overload kicks in after five: the brain simply cannot consciously process more than five concurrent inputs. Go for the five things you feel most motivated about and which you agree will make the most positive impact on your boss's achievements.

4. Make sure you align with your boss! Start by asking to see a copy of their objectives and use that to inform where you should focus your energy.

5. Keep the objectives SMART: Specific, Measurable, Agreed, Relevant and Timebound. The more concrete and granular the objective, the more likely it is to work. So "improve communication with sales team" would be much better as "meet with sales team to identify three agreed methods of improving communication and implement by June 2019".

6. Treat them as organic. Rarely, if ever, will an objective agreed in December still be relevant 12 months later. Chances are you will have achieved it or things will have changed and it is no longer relevant. Bring the document with you to your one-to-one reviews and keep updating it: insert new ones when you achieve one, amend and update as necessary.

7. Keep them visible. Physically put these five initiatives where you see them regularly. I have mine printed out and stuck to the pen holder on my desk. My kids used to print them and put them on their bedroom wall. It works.

I get to see copies of people's objectives quite often and I am constantly surprised at how many are meaningless, not even objectives. May I suggest you check yours out? Give them to someone else to read. If they're unclear, outdated or irrelevant, have a one-to-one meeting with your manager and suggest your amendments. No reasonable boss is going to shut that down. Objectives are designed to lift performance, so if you want to improve their quality it is probably going to benefit the business. And being proactive and showing leadership on this would be viewed by most people as a positive thing and thus will enhance your working relationship.

Where to start?

You're probably not going to have time to work on every relationship in your network. You need to prioritise: one way would be to look at the benefit versus the effort required to build the relationship. Something along the lines of this relationship planner (sounds terribly cynical, doesn't it?) would help you identify who's in the No-Brainer Quick Wins box: people where making this investment is important because of the impact they have in your working life, and where it is feasible for you to achieve this improvement. I'd be tempted to start by identifying three people in the top-right box.

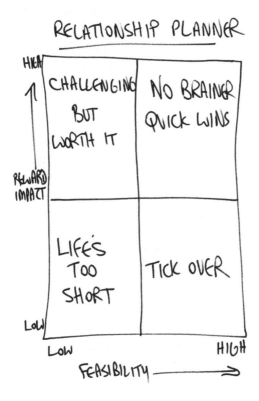

RELATIONSHIP PLANNER

HIGH

CHALLENGING BUT WORTH IT

NO BRAINER QUICK WINS

REWARD IMPACT

LIFE'S TOO SHORT

TICK OVER

LOW

LOW — FEASIBILITY — HIGH

A plea for more humanity

The chapter in which I propose investing more time in important relationships seems like the right place to wave the flag for all of us to do what we can to counteract the toxic erosion in relationships that is all around us. Throughout the book I quote examples of what I observe in the way human beings are losing sight of what's important.

We only get one go at this journey, so why don't we all try to do more to make it more meaningful and worthwhile by doing it alongside our fellow humans? Why don't we allow more time to check in with people at the beginning of a meeting – to celebrate a success or acknowledge and empathise with someone else's difficulties? Why don't we treat our break at lunchtime as an opportunity to catch up with a colleague we haven't seen for a while? Or to pick up the phone and talk to someone who helped us out a while back and has since gone quiet?

It's very easy to find a reason not to do these things. There will always be unanswered emails to handle, and just as the world will never stop spinning, so the great wheels of commerce will also never stop turning. It's a matter of making the effort, creating a bit of space for each other and putting more of a value on staying connected. Just because no one measures this and it goes on behind the scenes is no reason not to do it. If were all to adopt a more abundant mindset and be just a bit more generous with ourselves and our time, perhaps society might rebalance itself a little.

Summary

I hope you are now thinking about how to make building some important relationships more of a priority. I've always thought that if you get the relationship right with someone, you have more wiggle room when, as is inevitable, things go wrong on the detail. As we'll see in the next chapter, this is well proven when it comes to negotiating, and it holds true in general. Trust lies at the heart of it, and it is very hard to trust someone if you feel you don't know them.

Try keeping this chapter at the front of your mind for a couple of months and see where it takes you. Good luck!

Questions

- Where are you going to start?

- How will this benefit you if it works?

- What has been stopping you in the past?

- Who else can help you with this?

Make some notes on actions you can take to get started.

Tool 5. Negotiate for yourself

"God grant me the serenity to accept the things I cannot change, courage to change the things I can, and wisdom to know the difference."

Reinhold Neibuhr

Indeed Smithers, there is a good time to request a pay rise and this isn't it.

Introduction

One of the biggest barriers to a well-functioning career mojo is unwillingness or inability to negotiate successfully. If you operate on the premise, as I do, that most transactions with another person are a form of negotiation, then negotiating is a critical life skill. Surprisingly few people have been taught how to do it, in my experience, so this chapter is designed to even up the playing field in your favour.

The good news is that successful negotiation is not so much about technique as it is about mindset, so with a few adjustments it could well be that a whole bunch of better outcomes is available to you, potentially of life-changing importance.

A few guiding principles

Before we introduce any tools, let's establish a few guiding principles which I have found to be helpful over the years.

1. Not everything is negotiable. You can negotiate a lot more than you might think, but I disagree with the title of Gavin Kennedy's book *Everything is negotiable*.[39] With 36 years of happy marriage behind me I would not dream of negotiating fidelity or loyalty. But things are a lot more negotiable than you probably tell yourself.

2. It is a waste of time trying to negotiate that which is non-negotiable. Better to put your energy into battles you have a possibility of winning.

3. Negotiation is something you have to practise. It's like a muscle – it goes flabby when you don't use it. The more you use it, the easier and more fluent it becomes.

4. If you negotiate well, it improves relationships. Some people shy away from it because they fear it will make them unpopular. The opposite is the case.

5. If you don't bother to test other people's positions, you are often leaving opportunities on the table because very often the other person doesn't expect you to agree immediately.

6. Negotiation is a critical skill without which you are unlikely to achieve your full potential. It's not possible to function effectively at work without deploying it.

7. There is risk involved. Not saying "yes" to the unreasonable demand at the first opportunity and instead exploring alternative options takes courage and may meet with a bad reaction. However, the rewards it offers should more than compensate.

Why don't we negotiate more?

People tell me all the time that they don't negotiate because to do so would have them marked down as "being difficult". It's far easier to keep your head below the parapet and just get on with the job, for better or for worse.

In other words, it's self-talk. You tell yourself that negotiating means being difficult and so you don't do it.

Let's try turning that belief on its head and tell ourselves that negotiating is being helpful and that it is a form of leadership which is required of all of us. If you negotiate well and are looking for win/win outcomes, the other party will benefit as well. Not only that, you'll get a better relationship with them for the future, so it's a great skill to add to the toolkit for Tool 4 (Invest in relationships).

Let me share a personal example to illustrate the point.

I have to work hard at negotiating. I can do it very successfully, but it doesn't come naturally to me as I have an instinctive preference for being helpful towards others, often at my own expense. So when I do it, I have to dig deep. It can be uncomfortable for me, but I know there are times when I have no choice.

One such instance was when I was working with a client on developing a new training workshop which they planned to roll out across Europe. The topic was matrix management and the plan was to pilot the workshop with the executive team and then roll it out.

As we were developing the content of the workshop, my client, the HR manager, was asking for more and more technical content. He wanted more knowledge to be crammed in, so that the session was becoming more like a presentation. I was growing uncomfortable but carried on doing as he requested. Things got worse and worse, until eventually he rang me three days before the executive workshop and said he wanted me to fly out over the weekend to meet a matrix management specialist he had found, who could brief me on yet more content so that we could beef it up still further.

I realised I had no choice but to assert myself and get negotiating. I heard myself saying: "We have now reached a point where I no longer feel comfortable with the content of the workshop. If you insist on adding more detail, I strongly believe the workshop will fail, which will be very bad for me and possibly even worse for you, and I am not prepared to let that happen. Either we go with what we have agreed or I am afraid I will have to walk away from this project."

There was a bit of a stunned silence at the other end of the phone, before he said he would go with the workshop as planned. Needless to say, it went very well and everyone was happy. We arrived at a win/win which would otherwise have been a lose/lose. Not only that, but our relationship thereafter was on a totally different level. He respected me more and we were able to collaborate much more successfully. The Parent–Child became Adult–Adult, through me having the courage to say no. A strong lesson, and one which I keep in mind when working with clients and other key stakeholders.

What if we don't negotiate?

I meet people all the time who recognise that they need to negotiate more. The result is that they are wasting time, causing themselves stress and in some cases seeing the effects ruin their life outside of work.

You may remember that earlier in the book I mentioned that my research has shown that people waste three days per week doing things they shouldn't be doing, or doing things badly. If you don't negotiate, this situation doesn't change. You attend meetings you know are a waste of time because you didn't negotiate. You take on work you know you shouldn't because you don't negotiate. You say yes to things which impinge upon your personal time because you don't negotiate.

I remember following up with someone who'd attended one of my leadership courses. She said that now she had started negotiating she had managed to find time to have dinner with her husband every evening instead of just at weekends. Oh my goodness! How long had that been allowed to eat at her personal life?

Someone else told me recently that because he now negotiates which meetings he is attending (saying no to those with no agenda or which are not relevant to him), he has regained one day per week, during which he coaches his team, so that he has less hands-on work to do himself. This has transformed his experience of being at work.

Ultimately this is a choice, and we need to apply good decision making in order to allow ourselves to negotiate more.

It's all in the mind!

As I mentioned earlier, good negotiation is more about mindset than it is about technique. Let's have a go at demonstrating that.

I'm going to share a real-life experience with you. Let's see how you would have handled it.

> It was a cold night in February and I was staying in a fancy hotel in Edinburgh. At 3am the fire alarms went off, so I threw on a few clothes and went outside to stand on the frosty pavement for 30 minutes while the fire brigade established it was a false alarm. I went back to bed and didn't get back to sleep.
>
> At 7am I got up and discovered there was no hot water, so it was a cold shower and a cold shave to start the day. I was not a happy bunny.

What would you, honestly, have said when you went to check out that morning?

I use this exercise when I run negotiation courses, and I can tell you that the range of responses goes from:

- Nothing, I'd just never use that hotel again

  through to

- Ask for a £50 refund

  through to

- Refuse to pay anything and demand a voucher for a future stay to compensate for my inconvenience.

  The range of what I call "mental limits" on this particular

scenario is £0 through to £300.

Those mental limits – the voice that tells you what something is worth, or indeed whether something is negotiable – are self-imposed. You acquire your mental limits, maybe from seeing how others around you negotiate, or your culture, or the type of work you do. Who knows where you get them – the point is, they inform the way you go about negotiating.

So here's the first negotiation tool to put in your toolkit. Recognise that your personal mental limits might be inhibiting you and so the best thing is to find out what the other person's mental limits are first. Because they are probably different from yours.

Kerrrching! This is what I did in the hotel that day.

> "Good morning, room 35 checking out please. You are probably aware there was no hot water this morning. I was wondering what you can do to put that right for me?"
>
> "I'm so sorry, Mr Brown, let me have a word with my colleague." (Scurries off, returns with duty manager – a good sign.)
>
> "Mr Brown, we do apologise, this always seems to happen when we have a fire alarm go off. I expect you'd like me to write off last night's bill?"

As my mental limits had been telling me my discomfort was worth a £50 voucher, I graciously accepted the £150 offered and departed. I should probably have said it was a good start, now what about the inconvenience?

The technique is therefore to ask questions to find out the other person's mental limit before you tell them yours. Obvious really, when you think about it.

An elegant and easy-to-remember way of summing this up

can be found in Stephen Covey's book *The 7 habits of highly effective people*.[40] Habit 5 is this:

"Seek first to understand, then to be understood."

I love that. Find out what you're dealing with, then respond. It's a no-brainer. It's worked so often for me over the years.

> I once had a client who was asking me to propose something his company had never bought before and which I had never supplied before. I had no idea what he thought it was worth. I knew I had to wait for him to tell me, which after an hour he eventually did. He thought it was worth four times what I did. Needless to say, I adjusted my response accordingly and we met halfway, to the satisfaction of both parties. If I had gone too fast and stated my position too soon, I would have left a large amount of money on the table.

The other technique worth trying is applying someone else's mental limits. Ask yourself, "What would (person with strong mental limits) say or do in this situation?" and then respond accordingly. I used to have a boss who would ask advertising agencies for what I thought were ludicrous levels of discount on advertising, so when they called me I would switch on my "Be like John" persona and lo and behold, I am asking for a 75% discount and getting it.

A final thought on mental limits: once you have decided what your position is going to be on something, add (or deduct) 20% further. You will often get it, once again proving your mental limits need to be revised.

Negotiating collaboratively

When we are trying to negotiate collaboratively and want the other party to feel good about the outcome, we need to get past defensive reactions so that we can explore things together. Therefore we need to use signals and language which help the other party not to feel threatened.

Caroline Webb has some great advice on this in her excellent book *How to have a good day*.[41] She draws on cutting-edge research from behavioural economics, psychology and neuroscience, and is full of practical tips to make life easier. Here's her advice on this:

> *"We've escaped the rough-and tumble of our ancestors' lives on the savannah, but our survival circuits are still working just as hard to protect us in today's polished professional world. Our brain reacts just as quickly to personal affronts and work-place indignities as it does to genuine physical threats."*

She goes on to explain the difference between our brain's "discovery mode", when we are thinking deliberately and consciously, and "defensive mode", when the instinctive brain takes over and our response is fight, flight or freeze. When we make our approach to negotiate, we want to avoid triggering a defensive response if we possibly can.

According to Webb, the triggers to watch out for include social needs such as Inclusion (not being isolated or excluded in some way), Fairness and Respect, along with individual needs such as Autonomy, Competence (not feeling out of one's depth), Purpose (not violating one's personal values or what they deem to be important principles) and Security. The book then suggests ways to overcome these. If, when you approach the other person and don't take account of these social and individual needs, you will probably elicit a defensive response, and you'll find it hard to collaborate.

My suggestion is that you make a real effort to acknowledge the other person and recognise that they may have a different view of the world to yours. Create an atmosphere of collaboration based on mutual respect by making it obvious you are acknowledging them as well. You can signal this with some of the language you use:

"I completely understand why you might feel that way."

"Please tell me more about why you think that."

"Thank you for being so upfront about this."

Once you acknowledge the other person, it takes the heat out of the situation and both parties can move into Discovery mode. Use lots of open questions to get the other party talking, and when you have what you think is a good grasp of their perspective, offer a well-signalled summary to demonstrate that you have been listening and to remove any misunderstandings.

"Let me see if I have understood you correctly. You are asking me to come in again this weekend to help us catch up on the project. You don't think there is anyone else you could ask as this needs my specific input, and you are aware this is the third time you have asked me to do this. Have I missed anything, or is this a good summary of the situation?"

(The added benefit of this type of summary is that if it is a negotiation about something unreasonable, the other party gets to hear the unreasonable request for themselves and it might cause them to rethink it as you are playing it back to them. It is also buying you some time to calm down and start thinking straight again.)

Handling objections

The acknowledgement technique works very well when you are thrown an objection. This might be in a negotiation or when you are pitching an idea in a meeting. Objections are a good thing, by the way, as they show the other party is listening and is still engaged. I like to think of them as buying signals, and they are not something you need to squash immediately, but instead turn them into opportunities to close the sale.

My three-step approach to handling an objection is:

PAUSE – ACKNOWLEDGE – PROBE

Pause is good because it gives you a moment to think and stop yourself going into defensive mode. It's also hard to think and talk at the same time.

Acknowledge is good, for all the reasons above. It defuses the objection and builds respect. People who show respect usually get it back.

Probe involves asking open questions to try to find out what lies at the heart of the objection. Some great questions to ask are:

- What makes you say that?
- What would I have to do to have you sign this off?
- What do you suggest?
- How much of an issue is this?
- How much of a concern is it?
- If we can satisfy you on this, do we have a deal?

Let's try an example. A classic objection when you are selling something is, of course, price.

"I like it but it's too expensive."

(I pause before responding.)

"I understand, price is obviously a key consideration when buying a washing machine. Do you mind if I ask – when you say it's too expensive, what do you mean?"

"Well, it's £250 more than the other model over there, which has pretty much the same features."

"Yes, indeed it is. You mentioned that you like this one, even though the other one has, as you say, pretty much the same features. Why is that?"

"I prefer this brand. We owned one before and it lasted 15 years, so we feel we would prefer this one."

"Great, thank you for that. That's probably why this one costs more – the quality of the parts they use is higher. So how much of an issue is the £250?"

"Well, it's just that we can't afford it."

"I see. When you say you can't afford it, what does that actually mean?"

"Well, I can't afford it until I get my next pay cheque, which is two weeks away."

"OK, so if we fast forward to the end of the month, you are saying you'd be happy to buy it then?"

"Sure."

"So if we do the deal today and you leave a deposit and we invoice you the balance on 30-days terms, would that work for you?"

"It would indeed."

Try this tool next time you run into an objection. Don't try to kill it, P-A-P it.

Creative negotiating

When you are trying to negotiate on things which affect your mojo (workload, processes and procedures, roles and responsibilities, pay and reward and so on), you will probably be negotiating with someone with whom you have an ongoing relationship. Therefore win/win is probably the best mode to be in. Win/lose is unlikely to be a good mode because if you get what you want and they don't, you may damage the relationship and they may get you back later. People have long memories.

Finding a win/win requires two ingredients: courage and creativity. Courage because we need to engage in what is not always an easy conversation, and many people simply don't like negotiating. Creativity because win/win is not always obvious and we may have to think outside the box a bit.

Here's a tool to help with creativity. I call it the Deal Juggler. There are four devices to help you find creative answers to your negotiation. Let's use negotiating a salary increase as an example to explain the tool. (This one seems to pop up regularly on my negotiation courses. Can't think why.)

You haven't had a salary increase for three years and are trying to negotiate a 5% increase starting next month. You have reached an impasse – the boss has said there is nothing she can do as her salary increase budget has already been used up for the year. Whip out your Deal Juggler and try one of these:

1. Make it smaller. Instead of negotiating an increase for the next 12 months, see whether you can agree an interim increase (three-month maybe) by way of a project bonus, to tide you over until the next salary year when the budget becomes available again.

2. Make it bigger. Defer the increase until the next salary year but have it backdated to now and locked in for two successive years.

3. Change the mix. Add in some extra components. Talk about a mix of extra money, training, holiday, car allowance. These come out of different pots but they are all money.

4. Turn it upside down. Instead of talking about salary, talk about job role. Workload. Holiday. Pension. Bonus. Car. School fees. Maybe you can defer having a new company car next year and instead get more money. Maybe you can have two weeks' extra holiday as your daughter is getting married in Miami. You get the gist.

A simple but effective assertiveness tool

Mojo loss can occur when you aren't assertive enough to say what you really want to. Often what you want to say is "no" but you end up saying "yes" and then feel bad not only because you didn't get what you wanted but also because you didn't have the courage to say what you wanted.

I have to work on my assertiveness. I can do it, but my initial response when negotiating is to try to be helpful and popular. It's part of my personality, I guess, and it sometimes gets me into trouble.

I have learned various techniques to help me deal with this, one of which is to use a very short and simple word:

IF

Inserting "IF" into your response when someone asks you to do something turns it instantly into a negotiation. It can lead to much better outcomes.

One of my proudest moments when I got out of a tricky situation was on board a long-haul flight to San Francisco. I travel there regularly and I always travel economy. I often charge clients an all-inclusive fee for my work, so any expenses hit the profitability. I find it hard to justify another £2000 or more for a seat in which I know I will still not sleep, so I just put up with it for nine hours. But I do always nab a good seat, which on a British Airways 747 is seat 28D. This is an aisle seat at the front of the cabin, up against a bulkhead. Through the curtain is business class and there is no galley or toilet nearby. So there is no traffic going past and you can stick your legs out under the curtain. Perfect! I book it the minute the client confirms, often three months before I travel.

One day I boarded the flight and standing in front of my seat with his rucksack on it was a short, flustered-looking man and a woman and young child beside him.

"Is this your seat?" he said. "Yes, it is," I replied. "Would you mind swapping with me, so I can sit next to my wife and help her look after our child? They wouldn't let us sit next to each other when we checked in."

His seat was in the row behind, in the middle. The seat from hell.

The helpful man in me who doesn't like conflict wanted to say "yes, of course", but fortunately the logical bit of my brain took over and told me that if I said yes I would be cursing him for nine hours and he had no right to make his problem my problem. He could have requested better seats when he booked as they will accommodate people with small children in this way. So he had no excuse.

The hot flush came and went, and I recovered sufficiently to utter these immortal words:

"I can appreciate your problem. However, this is a good seat and I booked it months ago for a good reason, so I'm not prepared to let you have it. IF, on the other hand, you can find me the same legroom somewhere else on the plane, I'd be happy to help."

He looked daggers at me and slunk off to talk to the British Airways steward. He came back looking flushed and flung himself into the seat. I stuck in my headphones and tried to ignore the child clambering all over the seat next to me.

Ten minutes into the flight the BA steward came and knelt beside me and said, "Mr Brown, we've got a seat in business class if you'd like to come with me."

Win/win, and happiness unbounded for all. From a very simple "IF" statement.

Next time someone tries to get you to "swap seats" at work (i.e. give you their problem), try out the IF word.

"If I agree to do that for you, can you do this for me?" is in essence how it will play out.

"Can you get the report finished by Friday, Mike?" "Sure, if you can do the executive summary and are happy to do the slides for Monday."

Win/win involves a two-way street. IF helps you to make it two-way.

Giving yourself more power

If you have read any books on negotiation you have probably come across the word BATNA. It's an acronym for **B**est **A**lternative **T**o (a) **N**egotiated **A**greement. It's a non-word, impossible to visualise and thus hard to remember. I much prefer my version, which is BANANA. Visualise this when I suggest you always apply this principle when you negotiate:

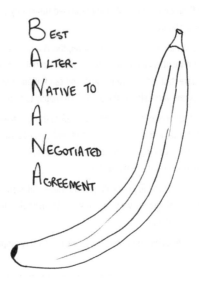

B est
A lter-
N ative to
A
N egotiated
A greement

Never negotiate without a BANANA in your pocket.

A BANANA is something you plan in advance – doing so will give you the option to walk away when you need to. It's the best alternative to doing a deal that day, with that person, on those terms.

Let's say you're buying a car. BANANAs you could plan in advance could include:

- Don't buy one at all. Do without till next year.
- Buy one from somewhere else.
- Buy a different model.
- Buy a motorbike instead.

If you don't have a BANANA in your pocket, you risk doing a deal you shouldn't do (because you have no alternative). You've probably been there – having no alternative but to accept the terms offered. It's not a comfortable feeling, and mentally you feel weak if you don't have that comfort of knowing it's OK to walk away. When you're negotiating for that last seat on the plane, that house that fulfils all your dreams and more and you need to move in before Christmas, that last puppy in the litter, you may not feel able to walk away, and the seller knows it.

So when you are negotiating and you need to get the best deal, spend a bit of time planning your opening position (aim 10% higher than you expect to achieve is a good rule of thumb) and know what your walk-away point should be – then work out your walk-away options. Do all of this and you will give yourself much more mental power – as I said before, it's all in the mind!

By the way, plastic BANANAS work, too. If they think you've got a BANANA, you've got a BANANA. Make sure they don't catch you out though.

Negotiation hints and tips

Let's finish with a few hints and tips which will help you to find more negotiation space in your job.

Firstly, try out the NOTHING FOR NOTHING mindset. Try not to give away anything for nothing. People don't value free stuff, so make it look expensive, using phrases such as "I'll have to have a think about that" or "I wouldn't normally, let me come back to you." Once people get used to asking for something in return when they approach you, they may turn their attention to someone else who might be less tricky to deal with!

Slow down your response. Allow a pause in the negotiation, so it looks as if you are weighing things up. Make notes, do come calculations. People will respect a "considered response" more than a quick one. It is also helpful because it gives you time to think and devise alternative options.

Recognise the power of Anchoring. This is about defining the negotiation playing field by going first with an aggressive opening offer. (If you're a softie like me, you have to plan this and put on a more assertive persona in order to pull this one off.) Research tells us that the deliberately low (or high, depending on whether you're buying or selling) offer will lead directly to better results for the person who opens the bidding.

What to do if someone low (or high) balls you? Respond quickly with an equally aggressive counter-bid. It balances the power in the equation. Or alternatively whip out your BANANA, assuming you have one (e.g. by walking away). It's a powerful response and may cajole the other party into not playing games with you.

Bear in mind when you negotiate that deep down humans all tend to want the same thing: they want to look good and to have an easy life. Think about how you can help them to sell your proposal and how you can make their life easier if they need to get approval from elsewhere. People don't want problems, they want solutions. Think it through from their perspective and show them how easy it will be for them to make the decision.

Summary

I have heard far too many examples over the years from people who have not negotiated where they could have and have lived to pay the price. It really is a choice as to whether or not you want to push back, test other people's positions, explore alternatives.

Working against us is the fact that negotiating takes time, and that is a scarce resource. Often the quickest thing is to just get on with it and leave negotiating for another day. That day then never comes, of course.

If your mojo really is fading, I urge you to give some of this a go. Even if you don't succeed in getting everything you want, you will have tried and you will have exercised that all-important negotiation muscle, and for both of those reasons you'll feel better.

Questions

- Where are you going to start negotiating?

- Which negotiation tools are you going to use?

- How will this benefit you if it works?

- What has been stopping you in the past?

- Who else can help you with this?

Make some notes on where you can get started.

Tool 6. Avoid avoidance

"It's not so difficult to comprehend why international skirmishes and violence occur, when we witness full-scale family warfare over putting down the toilet seat."

Thomas Crum

That's the boss's office. His door is always open for new staff.

Introduction

Conflict is a good thing. Without it there would be no learning, no change, no progress. The trouble is, not enough people see it that way. Conflict is viewed as something to be avoided because we worry about being seen as a troublemaker. This is a major source of corporate malfunction. It leads to the same mistakes being repeated over and over again, weak or non-existent levels of feedback, and huge amounts of time wasted in meetings where people are hiding or faking their response.

This chapter aims to encourage you to embrace conflict and feel better equipped to deal with it. This is your chance to break the mould and show others how dealing with conflict rather than avoiding it is a good thing. You'll all benefit if you can nail this one.

The avoidance default at work

One of the reasons you may not feel comfortable with conflict at work is the way others around you behave. Ralph Kilmann and Ken Thomas, who co-wrote the Thomas-Kilmann Conflict Mode Instrument (TKI) in 1971, have done research on this. For more than 40 years they have been working with organisations to identify how individuals prefer to deal with conflict. The five preferences are Competing, Collaborating, Compromising, Accommodating and Avoiding. Kilmann has established that in the workplace, Avoiding comes out as the preferred mode for resolving conflict. Interestingly, when people are asked to assess themselves outside of work, Avoiding is the least preferred mode.

A survey by the Centre for Effective Dispute Resolution in London, called "Tough times, tough talk", revealed that two-thirds of managers feel that their biggest challenge is holding difficult conversations and that only 44% feel they are effective at managing conflict.[42]

I have seen and heard evidence of this myself as I have worked with groups over the years. People tell me how infrequent feedback is, and how when it is given it is not specific enough to really mean anything. People avoid talking straight to each other. I heard from someone recently who told me he had been working with his manager for 18 months and had just received some negative feedback about his work relating to when they first started working together.

Project reviews don't take place regularly enough. Holding them with a client where a frank discussion of what went well and what didn't is a rarity. Usually people say this is because they don't have time for it, but when I press them on this, they often admit that fear of having a difficult conversation lies behind what is a missed opportunity to learn and in fact strengthen the relationship with the client.

I can think of two organisations I work with where they have measured how much they give away for free. Clients asked them to include some extra stuff into the scope of the project, which they should technically should have recharged. In both cases, the scope creep was nudging 30%. They were giving away nearly one-third more than they needed to because they avoided the supposedly "difficult" conversation (which probably wouldn't be "difficult" at all if handled properly).

I often run activities in the training room designed to expose how the group works as a team. Quite often the group fails to deliver on the mini project I have asked them to complete. When we come to review it and I ask who in the room thought the approach was wrong and they should have had a rethink, hands go up. "Why didn't you say something?" I ask. "I didn't want to hold the group back," they reply. Hmmm. So spotting an opportunity to improve and calling it when they see the group going down a rabbit hole is holding others back? Faulty thinking if ever I heard it, I'd say.

Several of my clients say one of their key strategic aims is to get closer to clients and have a much more consultative relationship with them. In one case they have been trying to do this for at least a decade. When we then analyse their culture and the way they handle conflict, we discover that they prefer either to avoid conflict or to deal with it by giving in – by being too helpful in the belief that this builds relationships. They will continue to fail to deliver their strategy as long as they continue not to be assertive and to not resolve systemic conflict in their relationships.

A diagnostic exercise

We are going to explore a model which will help you understand your response to conflict more fully. Before we do so, let me invite you to carry out a short exercise. I am not going to say anything about why we're doing it, as that might influence your response. Please take a metaphorical honesty tablet so that you respond to what comes next completely as yourself (not a version of yourself that you wish you were).

When you have taken the tablet, please turn the page and carry out the exercise. You will need a pencil (not a pen).

WRITE DOWN THE LEAST LAWFUL THING YOU HAVE EVER DONE

Note: speeding fines and parking tickets do not qualify.

Thank you. We will refer back to how you responded as we go through the next model.

The way you just responded to my instruction might be a useful indicator as to how you prefer to deal with conflict. The question I asked was a cheeky one, to say the least. Some might say inappropriate, rude, intrusive, risky. How did you respond?

A useful conflict model

Let's get the model onto the table. I alluded to it earlier. It's the world's most widely used conflict preferences model, known as the TKI. The model is based on the premise that we all have a personal preference for how we respond in a conflict situation. We are able to use our non-preferred response, but under pressure and in the heat of the moment, our preferred response is the most likely to present itself.

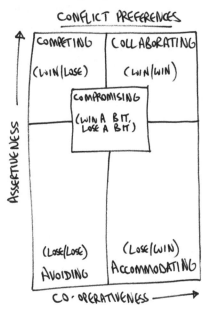

The model shows five conflict modes, each of which varies based on the extent to which, when under pressure, you are concerned with what other people need (Co-operativeness) or how much you are concerned with your own needs (Assertiveness).

Your preferences are organic: they evolve. You learn how to deal with conflict – from others around you, where you work, the nature of your work and so on. Maybe your boss encourages a certain style, or other styles are frowned on in your organisation. Chances are these might influence your personal "defaults" when there is conflict around.

Let's first try to work out what your preference is.

Remember the exercise we did five minutes ago on page 124? Let's see if it was your preference in action.

An Accommodator might have done as instructed but not felt terribly comfortable about it. Maybe wrote down a truthful answer that was in fact the least lawful thing they have ever done and glad they used a pencil so they can rub it out (because it's incriminating evidence!). Complied with my request because I issued it and I'm in charge here. Was that how you responded?

What about an Avoider? Maybe didn't do it at all, hoping that wouldn't spoil their understanding. Maybe wrote down something that wasn't true, or something that was unlawful but not the most unlawful thing they had ever done. Was this you?

A Competer might perhaps have proudly written down something that was true (maybe rather pleased with it as it was very naughty at the time, but no one found out and they got away with it) but knowing that under no circumstances would they share what they wrote down. They would meet the challenge from me, but have a plan for how to get the better of me if necessary.

A Compromiser is someone who likes to find workable solutions when there is conflict around but not spend all night over it. "It'll do – it's not perfect, but let's move on." So this person might have written something a bit illegal – something which might go along with the exercise in order to get the learning from it, but shying away from revealing the truly illegal thing they did 10 years ago. Working with me, but not revealing their complete hand. Might this have been your response?

And finally, the Collaborator. This person might have gone along with the exercise despite feeling uncomfortable because they were prepared to take a risk in order to get the maximum return from their investment. So they might have written down the truth but would draw the line if I said the next stage of the exercise is to email me what they wrote. If we'd been face to face, this person would have asked questions of the "what's in it for me?' type, and if satisfied that there was a benefit from taking the risk, would have been happy to do so.

It may or may not be the case that there is a link from this exercise to your conflict profile. Only you can answer that. If you think it helps you to assess what you think your profile is, that will be very helpful to us as we talk about the model in more detail.

Research has shown that as people develop and climb the corporate ladder, conflict preferences tend to climb up the model as well. In other words, people tend to become more comfortable with Competing and Collaborating over time. No real surprise: business leaders need to be OK with unpopular decisions at times (Competing) and need to be able to sit down and work out win/win solutions when the stakes are high and we need a long-term solution (Collaborating).

Collaborating is found in equal measure across both genders. However, males are significantly more competitive at all ages than females. (Dare I suggest no surprises there either?)

Consciously choosing which mode to be in for a given situation can be a great time saver, as well as helping to gear you up for dealing with conflicts that really do need to be resolved. We can make conscious choices about which mode to be in. Which one should we use when?

A time and place for all styles

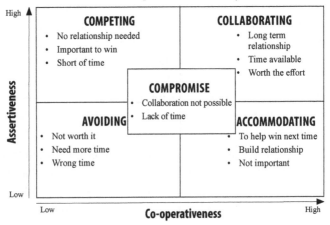

It can be OK to compete when you don't ever need to talk to the person again, or don't need to care about them. Bad salespeople tend to bring out the Competer in me, especially if they ring me at home on a Friday evening! Also if it is high stakes and I need to win. I might go Competitive if the house is on fire, or if someone is threatening my daughter.

Collaborating is a good idea when the stakes are high, we need to work together in future and I have the time to do so. One of the big downsides of Collaborating is that it takes time and energy. I probably won't bother to Collaborate when we are trying to agree which TV programme to watch. I should try to Collaborate when you, a key stakeholder, keep cancelling meetings at short notice.

This raises an important point about timing. If you need to have a Collaborative outcome on a high-stakes issue, start early. Allow plenty of time for it. It is very hard to Collaborate when you are pushed for time, and you may find you have to slip back to the next best thing, which is a Compromise outcome.

Compromise is a good choice when there is not enough time to do a Collaborative deal, or where perhaps it is not worth the effort. Meeting someone halfway can leave a slightly bad taste in the mouth, but it is better than no deal and we live to work together another day. Go for Compromise if you want to show that you are flexible as a means of building trust, but do it on issues where a real win/win is not crucial.

Accommodate when you want to build the relationship and it is low stakes. Let them have their way on something you don't need to worry about, so that you can build up your bank of points and cash them in later on high-stakes Collaborative issues. I would recommend that you sit down and work out which issues do not matter to you and you can use to build up this reserve of goodwill. The best issues to pick, of course, are the ones which have low cost to you and high perceived value to the other party. When you put them on the table, of course, you are going to make them look high cost to you, so that they are valued more highly by the other party. This is all basic negotiations stuff and no rocket science is involved. Use the appropriate body language to make it look painful (let your eyes fill with tears, wince a bit, sigh maybe. At times it's an act, especially if you are dealing with a cynical stakeholder who is doing the same to you).

A word of warning on the Accommodator response. Use it sparingly. If you do it too often it tends to make the other party think that you are going to Accommodate on everything, which can lead to them asking for more. Be a little unpredictable, and make sure they realise this is a one-off.

When is Avoiding a good choice? Not often. It does work in some situations:

- When you need more information ("let me come back to you").
- When emotions are running high ("let's take a break and talk again after lunch").
- When you know you can't win and can't afford to let someone else win. If you see no prospect of getting what you want, try to have the issue go away entirely (by being creative) so that no one ends up with it.

If you would like to complete the TKI profile, you can get in touch with OPP in Europe or CPP in the US. Alternatively, contact me and I can arrange to send you a copy and debrief it with you.

For a further explanation of the TKI and some online video content helping you to understand the different preferences, I made an 18-minute video on the topic which you can access here: https://youtu.be/u5atyrhVY1s

Using your self-awareness

Now that you have a better feel for your conflict preference, how do we use that information? I'd like to focus here on Avoiding and Accommodating, as these are the two profiles with most benefit to be gained by a change in behaviour.

In Tool 4 I introduced the Myers-Briggs® Type Indicator and got you thinking, among other things, about Introversion and Extraversion. Is your preference to have stimulation from contact with others (Extraversion) or do you get your energy from inside through being quiet (Introversion)?

Research tells us that Introversion maps onto Avoiding. Introverts tend to think before they talk, and it takes them more energy to say what's on their mind than Extraverts. Keeping your thoughts to yourself would seem to be a logical fit onto Avoiding, would it not?

Whatever the reason for having an Avoidance preference (and remember, this is organic: it evolves, and may well have been learned from watching how others around you handle conflict), the one thing I urge you to do is to avoid it. Avoid Avoidance! Why? Because conflict is like a seed: it grows. If you avoid a conflict, it sometimes goes away, but often doesn't. Then it gets bigger and before you know it, your seed is now a tree and needs a chainsaw to cut it down. Far better to pull it out when it's a seedling. Less stressful, and less agonising over when to do it.

This takes courage and is easier said than done. You may find it helpful to rehearse it in your mind, maybe even role play it with a friend. That difficult conversation could be a breakthrough, and whatever happens you know you will be able to congratulate yourself for having had a go, even if the result isn't perfect.

If Accommodating is your thing, my suggestion is to recognise when being helpful is not a good idea (it's usually when the matter is important and you feel you don't want to be as helpful as you usually are). Often people come to you to ask for things because they expect you to say yes (because you usually do). Once you start to ask more questions, explore things, not say yes straight away, they may realise you're not such a pushover and may stop asking you. Tool

5 (Negotiate for yourself) had more techniques which you can use here.

Coming back to what I said earlier about dealing with clients: not being so accommodating is a great way to get closer to a client because it involves them in having to explore joint options. Let's take an imaginary example. A client rings you and says they want you to produce the report two weeks earlier than previously agreed. If you Accommodate, you say yes to this and then spend the next weekend in the office with your team furiously working to meet the new deadline and hating the client for it.

If you Collaborate, you show you have understood the request, tell them that on the face of it that is not possible and ask some questions. This is the P-A-P approach to objection handling I talked about in Tool 5.

"Why do you need it one week earlier?"

"Because we would like to present it at the board meeting."

"Why do you want to present it at that meeting?"

"Because we might be able to get it into this year's budget if we do."

"Given that the full report won't be ready by then, how much information do you need to get the decision at that meeting?"

"Oh, an executive summary would be fine, actually."

"OK, if we produce an executive summary for you and maybe come along to take any questions they may have, how would that be?"

"Fantastic, even better in fact. Thanks."

Everybody happy, conflict defused and relationship improved.

Some other conflict handling tips

Here are some other tips people find helpful when dealing with conflict.

Ask questions. Using Covey's "Seek first to understand, then to be understood approach" I mentioned in Tool 5, I suggest you find out what you are dealing with before you pitch in. They may not see this as a conflict. They may see it is life threatening. Useful to know that before you tell them your position.

The questions you ask need to be open, so that you get the other party talking. These questions begin with WHO, WHAT, WHY, WHERE, WHEN and HOW?

Who says?

What room for manoeuvre do you have?

Why can't we do that?

Where does it say we're not allowed to?

When do you need it by?

How important is it?

As they talk, you are calming down, moving into Discovery mode and planning your options (while at the same time listening, of course). Then summarise what they said. This shows you listened, removes misunderstanding and allows you to take control.

Never respond if you have lost control. Maybe this person has flicked your switch and the red mist is descending. Hopefully this doesn't happen too often at work. Some people will deliberately insult you in order to have you lose control. If you feel this happening (increased heart rate, hot flush, shortness of breath), the chances are you will not respond as well as if you were in control. It will be the instinctive brain in control and you will respond as an animal with Fight, Flight or Freeze. If this happens, you are better getting out of the situation if you can. Put the phone down. Walk out of the room. By all means draft the email response, but save it, don't send it. I guarantee you when you read it the next morning, you will change it.

Talk straight. Be as clear and direct as you can. If you have bad news, don't dance around it and try to dress it up. Get to the point and move into exploration mode as quickly as you can. Try setting up the conversation before you hit them with it: "I have some bad news about the project. Not insurmountable, but we are going to have to do some expectation management. We've got a two-week delay."

Light relief: for a short video on how *not* to tell someone some bad news about the death of their pet, click on this link: www.youtube.com/watch?v=ZNyqEHp9JvU. The barely suppressed laughter throughout is because the video is entirely improvised and all Spencer knew when we started filming was that I was going to give him some bad news.

Finally, try out some aikido. Aikido is a Japanese martial art which focuses on harmonising with your opponent to bring peaceful resolutions to situations involving conflict. Its founder, Morihei Ueshiba, has this basic philosophy: "To injure an opponent is to injure yourself. To control aggression without inflicting injury is the Art of Peace."

This was suggested to me by an old school friend, who is now a Doctor, who wrote to me saying: "I think I learned a lot from 20 years of aikido where the practice is about never confronting. When I am seeing patients, this does not have to mean you are backing down. On the contrary, I win by agreeing then gently turning the direction of travel. I receive fewer bruises and my patients are generally pleased."

This approach comes back to the earlier point about avoiding the Defensive reaction. Trying to find a point of agreement and then going from there seems to be a positive approach.

Summary

I hope this chapter has encouraged you to face up to conflict more confidently. Speaking from experience as a natural Accommodator, I have learned over the years that I never regret having dealt with a conflict where I feel uncomfortable, and at times the benefits have been significant. I don't do it all the time, but I have learned to recognise when I need to break out of my preferred passive mode, and if I prepare myself well, I can do it.

Your mojo might well be considerably boosted from a healthy dose of conflict resolution and you will find that the more you make yourself do it, the more fluent it becomes and the bigger your comfort zone becomes. We all become more assertive as we get older, according to the research. This chapter has been designed to accelerate the process. I hope it works for you.

Questions

- What conflicts have you been avoiding?

- What have the consequences been?

- How will this benefit you if it works?

- What has been stopping you in the past?

- Who else can help you with this?

Make some notes on actions you can take to get started.

Tool 7. Think!

"It is not enough to be busy...the question is: what are we busy about?"

Henry David Thoreau

'Fail fast, fail often' seems to be one business mantra you two have taken to heart.

Introduction

I know you work hard. If you didn't you probably wouldn't be reading this book. Lazy people don't try to improve themselves, they try to find ways to avoid having to improve, such as getting other people to learn on their behalf. So that's not you.

Let's assume you are not looking for ways to work even harder. You are probably deeply tired and don't relax enough or take sufficient breaks. We need to work smarter, not harder. This chapter is designed to show you how.

"Thinking is for dummies!"

We live in a fast-paced world, and it's getting faster. We want answers, we want results and we want them NOW!

When I got my first job in 1980, if I wanted to send someone in a different department a written communication I would write it out longhand (with a pen) and give it to a person called a secretary to type. It was then brought back to me to sign (usually but not always the same day), put into an internal mail envelope and into a tray for the internal mail people to collect in a trolley. After a few days a reply would be delivered to my desk in another internal envelope when the man with the trolley reappeared. We still got things done, but the pace was undoubtedly slower.

Fast forward to today and there is an unwritten rule that you will be deluged with information and requests requiring your immediate attention, and you need to keep on top of these at all times. We live in a world of tiny attention spans, multi-tasking and incessant demands for our attention, making snap decisions and not thinking things through. Mistakes happen and we end up having to recover. This is the way to get things done the hard way. It can be, as someone said to me recently, "bleak, dark, tiring and very stressful". It can hurt your mojo.

I love what Frank Chimero says in his blog article about how complex we have made life (in this case in web design). The title of the article is "Everything easy is hard again":

"If knowledge about the web deteriorates quickly, it's worthwhile to develop a solid personal philosophy

toward change and learning. Silicon Valley has tried to provide a few of these. All are about speed. The most famous comes from Facebook, with their 'Move fast and break things' mantra. This phrase has been thrown under the bus enough times by now, but it is interesting that so few are willing to commit to its opposite: 'Go slow and fix things.' There are no limits to the amount of damage that can be inflicted by that dangerous cocktail of fast-moving-stupid."

It's not that mistakes in themselves are bad: in uncertain conditions, making mistakes can be a good thing, as long as we make them quickly and learn from them. As you probably know, this is the philosophy behind the Agile methodology, which is gaining traction in areas such as performance management as well as project management and business analysis.

But that's not a reason to tolerate unnecessary or sloppy mistakes. Most of the time, for most people, doing things right first time saves time and reduces stress. So how come we don't engage our brains and do more thinking for ourselves?

Maybe it's cultural. According to Nancy Kline in her excellent book *Time to think*, thinking is not a popular activity. "Thinking for yourself is regarded with suspicion. Some institutions thwart it on purpose. It can be seen as dangerous."[43]

Instead we learn to work out what we are supposed to think so that we can keep in favour with our bosses. And if someone is looking for help, we also learn that the correct response is to be the expert and do the thinking for them – a sure way to guarantee that the person looking for help will not learn, and indeed may end up feeling insulted, or at best turned into a helpless child. People become scared of having their own thoughts, at a time when organisations are screaming out for innovation.

Another factor which works against us is that even when we think we're thinking, we're screwing it up anyway, simply because human beings are so awful at making logical decisions. The definitive book to read on how the human brain works is Nobel Prize winner Daniel Kahneman's *Thinking fast and slow*.[44] In it he proves just how irrational our decision making is, through regularly getting the reader to consider two decision-making options and then decide on the best one. Time and time again, even though you know he is making the point about irrational decision making, he proves you wrong.

I'm not going to go into this in any more detail, I just want to make the point. When you think you're being terribly grown up and rational about things, you probably aren't. Here's an example from the book:

"A few years ago, supermarket shoppers in Sioux, Iowa encountered a sales promotion for Campbell's soup at about 10% off the regular price. On some days, a sign on the shelf said LIMIT OF 12 CANS PER PERSON. On other days the sign said NO LIMIT PER PERSON. Shoppers purchased an average of 7 cans when the limit was in force, twice as many as were bought when the limit was removed."

This is the effect of what is known as Anchoring, along with the rush of adrenaline the hunter gatherers in the shop feel when they suspect something is becoming scarce, and there is some urgency in the situation. This is not logical decision making, it is reptilian behaviour, and we display it each and every day. I don't have an answer for how to prevent it right here: I just want to remind you of its prevalence. We are not so smart as we like to think we are. As my wife constantly reminds me.

Three steps to getting things done

At the close of one of my workshops I was once asked by a senior director of a large global organisation what one model I thought had potential to make most difference to the bottom line. I looked around the room and walked him over to where I had drawn this diagram on a flipchart. I call the model Working Smart.

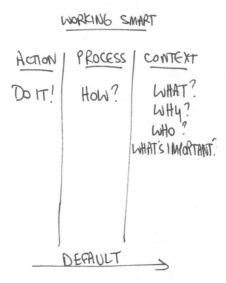

There are three steps to getting things done: doing it (ACTION), working out how to do it (PROCESS) and clarifying what we are supposed to be doing and why (CONTEXT).

The error made all too often, leading to not getting it right first time, is to start on the left-hand side of the model and work to the right. We use "the sooner we start, the sooner we'll finish" mentality to jump straight into action by starting with the ACTION step, working out how to do the project as we go along and not bothering to check what exactly we are supposed to do or why until we finish (if at all).

This is the equivalent of jumping out of an airplane and working out how to open the parachute on the way down. It's exciting but risky and somewhat stressful. It can lead to having to do things twice (because we misunderstood the brief) and can damage relationships, credibility and trust (especially if you do it to a customer). Some organisations are good at this. They almost pride themselves on it. "Thinking is for dummies. How difficult can it be, we've done this before and we are experts in our field. We know what they want, let's not mess around talking." Hmmm.

The trouble is, we become almost hard-wired to operate like this. We allow our adaptive unconscious mind to leap to conclusions – something that Malcolm Gladwell explains so well in his book *Blink: the power of thinking without thinking.*[45] We don't give the conscious mind enough time to work things out. Why? Because we are *always* up against time pressure, because time is money. It's peer pressure, too: everyone else operates like this and we don't have the courage to say, "Hold on a minute, let's think this through." People don't have time to think about what they're doing because they are too busy doing it. Urgency has taken over and we have become headless chickens.

I see this default behaviour wherever I work. Without exception.

For instance, I often use an exercise at the beginning of a workshop in which I give the group 15 minutes to obtain the answers to six questions from everyone in the room and capture them on a flipchart, using as much interaction as possible. I put up a slide with the exercise brief on it, explaining what I want them to do. I invite them to check anything they want to with me before they start; they rarely do. Usually someone is out of their seat before I have finished speaking.

Almost invariably they mess it up. Here's how:

"Get the information from **everyone in the room**"	*They NEVER ask me for my information and therefore don't include everyone in the room.*
"As you do this, interact as much as possible with each other"	*They usually use a process involving minimum interaction; in fact, it is often done in silence.*
"Design the process before you start"	*They design it as they go along, or don't design it at all and end up with several processes at the same time.*
"Make it user friendly so we can refer to it during the rest of the workshop"	*They ALWAYS ignore this.*

When we debrief and I ask them why they messed up on so many levels, they say:

"We assumed we knew what you wanted."

"We didn't plan it because you only gave us 15 minutes."

"We went with the first idea because we didn't have much time." Etc., etc.

Usually someone admits to having concerns about the way they were doing the exercise, but keeping their thoughts to themselves. Why? "Because we didn't know each other very well." How often do you work with people you don't know very well? "All the time." Hmmm.

This is not just a large corporate malaise either. I think it's societal and has crept into our way of functioning as humans. The popularity of such techniques as mindfulness is a response to this – an attempt to fight back against this tide of working too fast.

We can indeed get more done by slowing down.

The Working Smart model is great for meetings, and for projects of course, and it works superbly when negotiating. If you get the Context stage right when you negotiate (for instance, in establishing Trust), you'll find you can be less strong on price or quality and still win the deal. If they want to collaborate with you because you have the best relationship, you earn yourself more points and will beat the competition.

The key to Working Smart is to read my diagram as if it were Hebrew, starting on the right and working to the left. Let's explore this in more detail.

What (and how) to clarify at the start: Step 1

The CONTEXT stage is where we clarify the important things so that we can get it right first time. Here's a checklist (it's not exhaustive – add your own points):

- What are we doing? (Not as silly as it sounds. Do not proceed until you have answered this.)
- Why are we doing this? (Not always a popular question – the answer might be "we're not sure", or it might expose that someone should have asked this earlier.)
- Who's it for? (Know your customer.)
- What's important? (What criteria will the customer use to evaluate it?)
- How will it be used? (Who is the customer's customer and what do they care about?)

- What resources do we have? (Who's done it before, who has ideas?)

How do you respond to the idea of asking these questions? Some people tell me they resist them at first, partly because they sound a bit simple or even childlike. I agree, they are childlike, but in my experience, eight year olds ask the best questions. Asking questions like these is a way of putting aside your assumptions and accumulated expertise and bringing an open mind to the task. If instead of showing how experienced and clever you are you put your vulnerability out there (the possibility that you do not know the answer), you are being a leader. You are asking questions for which others may (possibly secretly) thank you. You are providing crucial facilitation to the group, and helping others to save time and Work Smart.

Another reason for not asking these questions is the fear of being seen as "difficult". One way to overcome this is to explain why you are asking and for it not to sound like an attack on anyone: "There's something I'm not clear on here, do you mind if I just ask for the sake of my understanding: why are we doing this?" Simply blurting out "Why are we doing this?" might be seen as being difficult and attract a defensive response from others. We want to encourage open minds all round, so position your questions in a collaborative way.

Agreeing your Process: Step 2

Do not proceed to Step 2 (the PROCESS stage) until you are all happy that you have answers to the Context questions.

Here you are going to agree HOW to go about the project. You know WHAT you're going to do, now work out HOW.

Again you don't have to be the project leader to pose this question. It can sound quite inoffensive and you can ask it as a member of the group:

"How do we think we should go about this?"

Brainstorm some options. Try not to run with the first idea in the interest of saving time. If someone wants to push on to the Action (Doing it) stage, hold them back:

"Just before we do that, let's check to see if anyone else has an alternative suggestion."

Once you have a Process in mind, check back to Step 1 to make sure that it ties in to all the information you have about the requirement. Then move on to Step 3.

At last! ACTION: Step 3

This is the favourite stage. Why? Because it's the sweet spot. It's where our expertise kicks in and where we feel as though at last we are making progress. This bit is measurable and we begin to see some outputs. We're good at this bit, and it's what we were hired to do. (None of us was asked to think about soft, fluffy stuff like Process, right?) It's where the adrenaline starts to flow, and to be honest, it's the easy bit.

At least using my approach you'll be beavering away safe in the knowledge that you are beavering on the right lake, and that you should be beavering and not squirrelling.

A final point to make about Working Smart: once you get into the ACTION stage, don't stay locked into it. Go back to Step 2 now and then to check your Process is still fit for purpose. If it isn't, check against Step 1 and see whether you need to adapt the Process. Perhaps things have changed, or maybe you now know more: modify the Process accordingly. Now that is what I call Agile working.

Use your ears as well as your brains

This tool is suggesting increased use of questions to help you waste less time, thus creating more space for other important things. If you start to ask more questions as you work on projects, you are using a God-given asset more effectively. You have two ears and one mouth, and using them in that ratio is a habit worth developing.

Think of yourself as an unofficial consultant. You can help other people to cope with their work by asking more questions, clarifying requirements and ensuring that you are working on the right things. Remember what I said in the introduction to the book? My research tells me that we spend only 40% of the working week doing Right activity – things which add value and are important. So much time is wasted because people do not ask enough questions. If you take the lead and develop a more consultative role within your organisation, you will be doing other people a favour at the same time.

People love being understood by others. It's ultimately all a customer really cares about, and let's face it, everyone has customers. Getting close to a customer and having a deep insight into what is important to them is, in my experience, a rare talent. What I have seen over the years is a tendency for salespeople to not want to get too close to customers. There is almost a sense of seeing how quickly I can get off the call or out of the meeting. Let me ask a few questions to find out what they want, and if I think I can provide it I will take the order and get out of there.

This is transactional, and a missed opportunity. If you understand someone's real context you can build a deep and lasting relationship. If you're a salesperson, it can transform your numbers.

I met Peter on a sales development workshop I was running for an energy consultancy in London. We covered my Working Smart model and worked on how to ask good questions. A couple of months later I was back in the same office and I bumped into him in the corridor. "Oi! Mate, I've got a bone to pick with you," he drawled in his Aussie accent. "You didn't tell me that when I started asking these questions I was going to get so damn busy!"

Intrigued, I asked him to elaborate.

"I took a call a few weeks ago from someone saying they wanted us to do a bespoke report for them on oil pricing in the Middle East, budget £50,000, could we do it? Instead of saying when did they need it and getting off the phone, I remembered to ask more questions to find out why they were asking and how it was going to be used. Turned out it was for a legal dispute over pricing and we ended up representing them in court and earning fees of £500,000."

Use the model to slow yourself down. Avoid jumping out of the airplane without checking your parachute and you could save yourself a lot of stress and build some great relationships. And even make more money. Woo hoo!

Summary

One symptom of a damaged career mojo is the belief that "thinking is for dummies". I have explained how slowing down and engaging the conscious mind will help not only you but the people you work with. Tool 7 is therefore the opposite: "Think!" It will cost you time at the start but pay off handsomely later. Well worth the investment.

Questions

- Where can you apply this model?

- Who else could you share it with?

- Can you introduce it on a project which is already under way?

- How might you use more questions to get closer to some key people?

Make some notes on actions you need to take if you recognise that you have not been working as smart as you might have.

Tool 8. Listen more, transmit less

"Don't talk unless you can improve the silence."
Proverb

So this morning we'll go round the table so
I can hear all your ideas before I tell you
what I've already decided we'll do.

Introduction

I said this before (in the previous chapter) and I'll say it again. We were born with two ears and one mouth. This is for a reason. Using our ears twice as much as our mouth will transform our relationships with others and unlock access to a whole new insight into opportunities you didn't know existed. Furthermore, genuine listening will build trust, and as we know from Tool 2, this will help both you and the other person.

Trouble is, it's not easy. It requires self-discipline, it takes time (although in the long term it saves it) and it requires us to pay genuine attention to other people. According to Nancy Kline:

"We think we listen but we don't. We finish each other's sentences, we interrupt each other, we moan together, we fill in the pauses with our own stories, we look at our watches, we sigh, frown, tap our finger, read the newspaper, or walk away. We give advice, advice, advice."[46]

She goes on in her book to describe another challenge, which is that we are conditioned to not listen. What she calls a Thinking Environment – one where people have a chance to fully express themselves and work out their own solutions – is a very different one from the default leadership style in most organisations, which is essentially the result of Male Conditioning. Nancy sums up the difference using this table:[47]

Thinking Environment	Male Conditioning
Listen	Take over and talk
Ask incisive questions	Know everything
Establish equality	Assume superiority
Appreciate	Criticise

Be at ease	Control
Encourage	Compete
Feel	Toughen
Supply accurate information	Lie
Humanise the place	Conquer the place
Create diversity	Deride difference

Stephen MR Covey uses the phrase "listen first".[48] He emphasises the need to listen before you try to diagnose or influence the other person. Otherwise you end up making assumptions, falling at the first hurdle, embarrassing yourself and potentially damaging the relationship.

> *"When I have interviews or when people come up to me with questions after a program or presentation, I find that, by far, Listen First is the behaviour I recommend most. It's the starting point in almost any situation. So often, problems people have, both at work and at home, are because they don't really listen first."*

Listening shows respect: you are able to acknowledge the other person, which is often all they want. Acknowledgement is a basic need for human beings; if you aren't being acknowledged; your mojo is probably malfunctioning.

This chapter is designed to get you thinking about where you could listen more and transmit less, and I have one or two tools to help you to do that.

The power of silence

We inhabit a world where there is a super-abundance of transmission, to the point of overwhelm. Twitter is the ultimate manifestation of this – a tool in which millions of us are in effect standing on a box shouting as loud as we can, in the hope that someone out there will hear us.

We're uncomfortable with silence. How often do you hear a lengthy pause during someone's presentation? The typical conference call has no pauses. An exhausting stream of transmission, with no punctuation marks. Don't stop talking otherwise someone will take the ball from you.

You can't think and talk at the same time. It's also hard to process what someone is saying while they're still talking. When you learn to shut up, you have a chance to understand. Mutual understanding is essential to good relationships, and as we've seen earlier, key to a healthy career mojo is the ability to build good relationships.

Let's look at how doing less of the talking could help boost your mojo.

The Introverts welcome it

Roughly 50% of us have a preference for Introversion – the Myers-Briggs® term for getting energy from inside rather than from outside stimuli. This fact is often overlooked by Extraverts, who welcome stimulation from outside. According to Susan Cain, whose book *Quiet: the power of the introvert in a world that can't stop talking* should be mandatory reading for all of us – Extraverts for its insight into the mind of Introverts, and Introverts for strategies for handling those noisy and disrespectful Extraverts – Introverts are literally wired differently to Extraverts.

> *"Introverts have the same physical nervous system as Extraverts, but they have a different sensitivity to stimuli. Their nervous system reacts more to all forms of stimulation. They work best where there is less stimulation. Extraverts do the opposite. They get listless and bored where there is not enough stimulation."*[49]

Extraverts think out loud and are happy to do the talking in meetings. Introverts tend to think about what they say before they say it and often need space to get their thoughts out – maybe via a second sentence. When an Extravert interrupts them or jumps in too quickly, the Introvert doesn't get their point across. Leading to misunderstandings and frustration and often disengagement by the Introvert.

I make training videos through a small business I set up a few years ago, which I run with training consultant mates Iain Smith and Spencer Holmes. Iain is an Extravert of the loud variety, as on occasions am I (especially when I'm with other loud Extraverts). Spencer is an Introvert. When we get together for one of our filming days or a rare face-to-face business meeting, Iain and I usually forget that Spencer is an Introvert. He tends to go along with all the noise and banter for a while, then you can see his energy fade and he visibly withdraws. This is a clue to us two to calm down and do some listening.

In the next chapter we'll see how to draw in Introverts during meetings. For now, if you're an Extravert, consider which of your key stakeholders is an Introvert and have a think about how to allow more space so you can access their contribution. If you're Introvert, how can you ensure your voice gets heard? Does someone need some feedback? Do you need to be more visible in meetings? Do you need to stop people from interrupting or ignoring you?

Remember, Introverts often have a different perspective because they think differently and can see things objectively because they're not talking so much. Just because they are quiet does *not* mean they don't have an opinion (sorry to disappoint you, my fellow Extraverts!).

It helps others to grow

What are you looking for from your manager? What's the number one attribute you'd like to see in her?

Google researched this question extensively in 2013 in what they called Project Oxygen.[50] From thousands of internal interviews with engineering managers and their teams they discovered that the number one thing people are looking for in their manager was them being a good coach. Ponder that for a moment. Are you just a little surprised by it?

Running a close second came "Empowers me. Does not micromanage". At the bottom of the list of eight qualities was "Has key technical skills". This is the opposite of what most people expect and implies a complete rethink of how managers should prioritise their time. If you're a manager, how much of a priority are you making coaching? Whatever your role, how much coaching do you get and what is the impact of that? If you're not getting enough, how much is that hitting your mojo?

I wonder what you make of this. It's a slide I use when the training topic is coaching.

When I ask you to listen and you start giving advice, you have not done what I have asked.

When I ask you to listen and you start telling me why I shouldn't feel the way I do, you are invalidating my feelings.

When I ask you to listen and you interrupt and start trying to solve my problem, I feel underestimated and disempowered.

When I ask you to listen and you start telling me what I need to do, I feel offended, pressured and controlled.

When I ask you to listen, it does not mean I am helpless.

I may be faltering, depressed or discouraged, but I am not helpless.

When I ask you to listen and you do things which I can and need to do for myself, you hurt my self-esteem.

But when you accept the way I feel, then I don't need to spend time and energy trying to defend myself or convince you, and I can focus on figuring out why I feel the way I feel and what to do about it.

And when I do that, I don't need advice, just support, trust and encouragement.

Please remember that what you think are irrational feelings always make sense if you take time to listen and understand me.

Coaching is not something you do only if you're a manager. We can all be coaches, and if we do it well we help others to grow while at the same time learning ourselves. Good coaching is rare, and I know of no organisation where managers see coaching as a priority. Not enough people know how to coach well, and the default coaching style I see people use can do more harm than good (as in the slide I reproduced above).

Too many people think when someone asks for coaching, their role is to problem solve and "fix" the coaching requirement as quickly as possible. They believe a good coaching session is a quick coaching session. Their preferred coaching style is Directive – making suggestions and locking in on the answer to the "problem" as soon as it has been defined, in the interest of saving time and doing what they think is required of them, which is to provide answers.

If you are finding yourself "in the weeds" at work, dealing with details that others ought to be dealing with themselves, it may be that part of the reason is these people have not been coached well, if at all. Providing answers for people disempowers them and causes them not to grow. In fact, it infantilises them and can lead to frustration or disengagement.

A great way to help people to step up and take on more responsibility is to coach them using a listening style. Caroline Webb describes this brilliantly:

"When someone is telling you about a problem and we leap in to offer advice, a paradox arises: it's all too easy to leave the other person feeling bombarded rather than soothed. 'Have you done this? What about that?' Inadvertently, we can even make the other person feel judged, as if they should have spotted the answer themselves. If that happens, their brain is likely to register our well-intentioned help as a kind of threat – which makes them less creative in their own thinking about the problem. By the end of the discussion, instead of saying, 'Wow, I feel motivated and empowered now,' they're mumbling, 'Well, I guess I'll go and do all those things then'." [51]

Avoiding this will involve asking some wonderfully simple questions, such as:

- Why is this important?
- What do you think?
- What have you tried so far?
- What are the options?
- What are you going to do differently?

Some of the best coaches I know are Introverts. They can be great coaches because they are more natural listeners.

Carrying on doing what has not worked previously is a form of madness, as they say. I wonder whether you are working hard doing things you shouldn't be, or not doing them particularly well (remember the Working Smart model in the previous chapter?) because of a lack of coaching. You not coaching others enough, or others not coaching you. Either way, if you think this is part of the story, what are you going to do about it?

Listening provides you with options

In previous chapters we have looked at negotiation and conflict handling. The core skill in both cases is the ability to listen and to ask good questions. In fact, research tells us that the most effective negotiators are those who talk least and ask the best questions.

I once ran a series of negotiations workshops with a company in Holland, in which negotiation role plays were the main activity to help people learn. We had a team of negotiators for the programme, playing the role of Procurement. The negotiator who got the best results for himself was an expert in saying virtually nothing. I was observing one of these role plays and remember it very well. It went something like this:

Harry: "Thank you very much for sending through your proposal. I was wondering what flexibility you have on the price."

Salesperson: "Oh, we could increase your discount level to 40%."

Harry: "That would be very helpful, thank you."

SILENCE

Salesperson: "I was also thinking we could add in some free training."

> Harry: "Excellent. Thank you."
>
> SILENCE
>
> Salesperson: "Would it help if we held our renewal price at this year's level for three years?"
>
> Harry: "It would."
>
> And so it carried on for another 10 minutes, concession after concession without Harry having to do much other than keep his mouth shut. A salutary lesson for the trainee salesperson.

An important technique here is to get the other person talking. Here are a few tips on how to do that:

- Defer to their expertise. "You have more experience of this than I do. What would be a reasonable timescale?"

- Set a range without making an offer. "I've heard that xyz is the going rate for this."

- Expose their underlying interests. "You have asked us to agree to the end of the month. Can you say more about why that is so important?"

- Funnel question. Ask them "why" several times in succession.

- Ask them to summarise. "What do you think we have agreed so far?" Or "How do you feel about the progress we are making?"

How do you listen?

Funny if you think about it. We get taught how to talk, read and write when we're young, but no one teaches us the other (and arguably most important) communication skill, which is how to listen. Pity really. The world might be a better place if we were better at it.

Firstly, let's be aware of why we are listening. We are listening to understand. Not listening to identify when there is a gap in the transmission so we can reply. Not listening in order to respond. Not listening in order to disagree. Our aim is to understand the other person's position in order to empathise and recognise our starting point for the conversation.

Caroline Webb has some good suggestions to make:[52]

- Let the other person set the topic (because it's about them, not you).
- Don't interrupt (SO hard!).
- Maintain eye contact. When you avert your eyes, even for a moment, it can break rapport.
- Keep them talking. Nod. Smile. Ask: "what else?"

Remember that Introverts sometimes need a few attempts at getting their thinking out. Pause to allow them time to go on to say more. This is often when they will say what's really on their mind.

If appropriate, make notes. Summarise: play it back to them and make it clear that this is to check your understanding. "If I've understood you correctly, you are saying…"

Create rapport. When you have rapport, both people will find it easier to communicate and to think. Match their posture, gestures, energy level, facial expressions. Match the volume of their voice and even the speed. Become like the other person by modifying yourself. Subconsciously the other person will find you easier to deal with because you are more like themselves. That will help both of you.

I was coaching someone recently who project manages software implementation teams in London. He is exhausted by his work, to the point of being ill. He told me: "I'm running so fast, I don't have time to involve the Introverts. Either they speak up or I will fill the space for them." He is missing out on a contribution that could transform his workplace experience, if only he could find a way to make time for it.

Summary

There's nothing new about the suggestion to listen more. You know it makes sense, as they say. Encouraging you to prioritise it and plan with whom you are going to really work on this might be a new idea. I absolutely acknowledge it is easier said than done. It is the area I am working on myself, and have been for several years now. There are times when I think I do it successfully and others where I evidently don't (my wife has one or two examples she could share to prove this point!). Unlearning old habits is much harder than developing new ones. The thing is to recognise it and make a start. I sincerely hope you will.

Questions

- Who do you need to listen to more?

- How can you make an opportunity for that?

- What might the benefits be?

Make some notes on actions you need to take.

Tool 9. Meet intelligently

"The single most important skill in meeting management is knowing what to leave out."

Kevan Hall, Speed Lead

It's been busy, everyone's tired so let's have a staff meeting!

Introduction

Let me guess. You spend at least 30% of your working week in meetings or on conference calls. If you're particularly unlucky this could be twice that. And how much of that is a good use of your time? Thought so. Not a lot.

You can probably predict where we're going with this chapter. It's not going to be about how to chair or lead meetings so much as it will be about how to be more intelligent about how to use that scarce and sacred resource – time. Ineffective and inappropriate meetings are, people tell me, their number one time stealer each and every week. Time you did something about that?

Note that we are talking about meetings which are designed to move things forward – get some decisions and some agreed actions. There are other types of meetings which are more of a "group hug": share some best practice, check in with each other, acknowledge some achievements, learn something new and walk away feeling motivated and inspired to carry on. These are a perfectly valid use of time and are not the object of scrutiny in this chapter.

Kevan Hall's book *Speed lead* has some excellent advice on what type of meeting to run based on the makeup and purpose of your team. Kevan breaks them into two types: "Star" and "Spaghetti" teams.[53] Read his book if you want to work out whether the agendas for your meetings are appropriate for your team. They often aren't.

What a waste of time!

Over the years various studies, including my own, have shown that there are high levels of dissatisfaction with meetings. Biggest causes of angst are:

- unclear objectives and poor or non-existent agendas, and therefore wandering off topic
- lack of self-discipline and mutual respect
- poor or non-existent timekeeping
- poor or non-existent preparation

- inappropriate use of time (e.g. presenting information which could and should have been circulated and read beforehand)
- unclear results, including decisions made and who does what
- lack of respect for others' time (including acknowledging time zones)
- irrelevance to attendees.

All of these are easily fixed – no rocket science involved. This really is a case of waking up and getting a grip, and not slipping into the dysfunctionality which others perpetrate. You will find that if you start to model a new way of running meetings, others begin to follow.

I once sat in on a client's meeting to give my observations. A group of learning and development specialists were having a quarterly review meeting. About 20 minutes into it someone had the courage to say: "Excuse me, would someone mind telling me what we are talking about, and why?"

Faces around the table indicated that other people were asking themselves the same question.

No agenda = no meeting!

Meetings without agendas are at best going to be inefficient and at worst a waste of time. If you provide a focus for the discussion you are able to keep people on topic and manage the time.

My first suggestion is that you do not attend meetings without agendas.

I repeat. Do not attend meetings without agendas.

Obviously the ones you organise are included in this. When you receive the meeting invite, ask what the agenda is. If there is none, you could ask for one, and if there is not one forthcoming, you can politely decline on the grounds that you do not know whether it is relevant to you. You can ask them to send you the minutes of the meeting so that you can decide whether to attend next time. There won't be any of those either, so you're in the clear!

I have numerous examples of people telling me that this one principle alone has saved them many hours each and every week – and guess what, the world is still spinning and they haven't been fired. In fact, they now have more time to think, to coach, to read, and they have recovered much of their mojo.

Give people time to provide input into the agenda before the meeting. That way they buy in and can give the items some thought before they come (very welcome by the Introverts).

Because the agenda is pre-agreed you are now able to shut down agenda hijackers. You know, the person who 10 minutes before the end of the meeting drops a bomb of some sort, which you don't have time to discuss properly and throws everything into confusion.

Example: "Guys, thought I ought to mention that Tom resigned last week so he won't be able to lead the project." Great! Thanks for telling us now, after we've been talking about the project for an hour.

If people don't have the discipline to ask for their item to be on the agenda, it doesn't get discussed. In other words, don't allow AOB (Any Other Business). We only allow Adults in these meetings.

Manage the time

Have you ever noticed how when you put a timescale on something people seem to work to it? This works very well with agendas. Put how long you are allowing for the topic on the agenda. And then appoint someone to be the timekeeper and ask them to interrupt when you are five minutes from the deadline. I promise you, it will focus people's minds.

Set the objective

As well as adding timing to the agenda, state an objective for the agenda item. "Decision required on how to achieve 5% budget savings next quarter. 15 minutes."

Then when Jasmine goes off on a personal moan about how unfair it is, you can bring her back to the objective and remind her of how long we have to get to our decision.

Capture the decisions and agreed actions

Meetings are designed to produce action. We need to capture what is agreed so that we can review progress next time. If people know that they are going to be held accountable it tends to make a difference to whether they do what they said they would. Here's how to make that happen.

I suggest you ask someone to take the minutes. They can do this during the meeting using a simple spreadsheet with four columns:

ITEM	ACTION	BY WHOM	BY WHEN
Expense budget cut	No foreign travel July or August	All	1 Sept

	Defer laptop replacement	John Paul Ringo	1 Jan 2019
Office move	Decide what colour carpet in Mike's office	Henry Mike	End July

This can then be circulated straight after the meeting.

And then, guess what, we are going to review this document as the first item on the agenda at our next meeting. If you chose to not do what you said you would, be ready to explain yourself next time.

The joy of having someone fill this out is that they can't do so unless things are clear. So they will have to ask, "Who is going to do this? When by?" before they can fill it in – a very useful way to refocus the discussion.

Encourage participation

When we invite people to a meeting the intention is generally to invite their contribution. (There can be other reasons, I suppose, such as to impress them, to bully them through sheer numbers, or to tick the political correctness box. But let's leave those to one side for now.)

Unless you are careful you will tend to have an imbalance in the contribution levels, often because the vocal ones get in first, excluding the more thoughtful or softly spoken ones (or those for whom the language for the meeting is not their first language and they are having to process everything twice).

There are several ways you can get around this. Nancy Kline suggests you kick off the meeting by asking *everyone* to say what is going well in their work or in the group's work.

This has the effect of creating a positive atmosphere in the meeting, which will allow people to think more creatively.[54]

When you start discussion of a topic, she suggests you give everyone a turn to input their ideas without interruption. Once people know that you are doing this, two things happen: people relax, knowing they will have their turn, and they also realise they are going to be required to contribute, so they had better be prepared to think and to remain engaged.

Nancy is a passionate advocate of not allowing interruptions. Once this is enforced, the benefits flow because people know they are going to be allowed to finish their thought. They don't have to anticipate interruptions, which means they don't feel a need to elaborate and can maintain their train of thought. Not interrupting will save time in the meeting. It also makes sense because often people need time to articulate their idea and can't get it over in just one sentence. And usually the meaning of their point is at the end of the sentence anyway, so if you interrupt you don't fully understand their point.

This device works well in virtual meetings, of course, and the fact that everyone knows they will be asked to contribute may make it more likely that they remain engaged rather than doing their email.

I recommend that you don't go round the table starting at one end and working round in sequence. This is what I call "creeping death", in that everyone knows whose turn is next and anxiety levels can rise accordingly. Much better to let people contribute when they're ready. Introverts may take longer to pump themselves up for the moment, whereas an Extravert is more likely to be happy to wade in at the start.

An alternative, fun way to manage contribution levels is to give everyone a paper cup and 10 paper clips. Every time they say something they have to put a clip in the cup. When they are out of clips, they are out of the conversation. You'd be surprised how this slows down the discussion and has people thinking much more carefully about whether to say something. You may need a "clip monitor" to ensure people stick by the rules. It can be a good exercise to do with a team which meets regularly and is a bit imbalanced with its air time. It makes the point without pointing any fingers.

Amazing, huh?

All of the above is, to my mind, absolutely basic common sense and good practice. Nothing new here whatsoever. Despite that, I am constantly amazed at the reaction I get when I introduce it in my training programmes. You see people taking copious notes and they seem a little startled at the suggestions I am making. Wow, really? That is how far we have come, folks, I'm afraid. We really have lost sight of some of the basics.

Are you facilitating or leading?

I hear a lot of confusion about facilitation and what it involves. People think they are facilitating when in fact they are leading. This can be damaging.

Facilitating involves helping a group to work out a solution to something. Leading involves, as the name suggests, leading the group towards a solution. Sometimes we need to put on both hats during a meeting. Of the two, facilitation is much more of an art form. It requires judgement and agile thinking.

I like to think of facilitating as being like a referee in a game of football (soccer if you prefer). Good referees are invisible when they can be and blow the whistle only when they need to. Crucially, they do not kick the ball!

It is the job of the two teams to play the game and abide by the rules (i.e. stick to the agenda or the agreed objective of the discussion). When they stop doing so, the referee needs to blow the whistle.

In other words, if you are facilitating, you do not have an opinion. You are there to facilitate the group in carrying out the task: to make it easy for them (the word has its roots in Latin, *facilis* – easy).

Once you stop having an opinion you will find it easier to observe the process the group is using and to help them when you need to. You create an Adult-to-Adult relationship with the group, as opposed to a Parent–Child one, which is often what you get when you lead a discussion.

Tip: as facilitator you do not have to be the person at the front holding the pen and writing everything down. You can delegate that, thus freeing yourself up to observe the "game" and check that the process is working.

Tip: whether it's you or someone else capturing the outputs on a whiteboard, make sure you write down what people say – not what you think they meant. If you distort their words into yours you are judging them and positioning yourself as a mind reader or an expert. Jim says "Redesign the process" and you write "Procurement rethink". There is no better way to upset them and create a Parent–Child relationship. Even if you don't understand it, and definitely even if you don't agree with it, write it down verbatim if you can. When you've finished writing it all down, you can review the list – if there is something ridiculous up there, normally someone in the group will spot it and call it out. You thus keep your healthy Adult relationship intact.

How to get things off to a flying start

Things often go wrong at the start of the meeting or the discussion. People aren't engaged, they don't know what's expected of them, they aren't sure what's coming.

It's time for me to wheel out my tried-and-tested model for getting off to a flying start. This works brilliantly in meetings and is also a great tool for kicking off a presentation. The idea is to clarify the five things that people need to know before they can get into the discussion (or listen to the presentation). So in your introduction you need to spell out, most conveniently, wait for it…

INTRO

You don't have to cover these in this order, but they do need to be covered.

I	INTEREST	Say something that will catch their attention. This could be a recent piece of news, the latest results/data on the topic, something someone important has said, an example of something relevant. "Let me read you this complaint I received yesterday." People will tune in and engage when you do this.
N	**NEED**	Point out to them why we are having this discussion. Some form of emotional appeal is always helpful here. Fear is a good one, as is excitement or pride. "If we don't decide today what to do the board will decide for us." "This is a chance to influence the redesign and make our lives easier."

T	**TIMING**	People worry about how long this is going to take. So tell them.
R	**ROUTE MAP**	They also worry about what is going to happen. What are we going to do and how are we going to do it? So tell them the agenda and how you're going to cover it. "We're going to look at the latest results, then brainstorm some ways to address the deficit, and then we'll agree who does what. I've got three slides I want to share first, which I'll send you afterwards. Johnnie is going to make notes and will send the minutes out afterwards."
O	**OBJECTIVE**	This is often not stated (ridiculously). "By the end of this discussion we need to have decided who gets promoted this year." "By the end of this presentation you will know the three main differences between versions 1.0 and 2.0." Keep this SMART, i.e. as concrete and measurable as possible.

You might want to prepare the INTRO in advance so you have something to say on each point. If it's a big presentation, write it out and practise it in front of a mirror (it normally takes only three or four sentences). Then when you stand up you just hit your mental "play" button and out will pop the perfect opening few words. They will be ready to engage and you'll have settled down. Perfect!

Summary

This has been the shortest chapter so far. Why? Because it's a very simple proposition. Do something about the dysfunctional meetings you sit in every day. It doesn't have to be your meeting – you can influence it by engaging with the meeting owner beforehand and influencing how it is organised. You can also use more assertiveness to push back on the time wasters. This is leadership and will, I hope, be encouraged by key players such as your boss, for instance.

Too often people have a meeting because they always have them on Mondays. Sometimes all you need to do is ask "Why?" "Because we always do" ought to be a chance to negotiate.

Final thought: we read at 450 words per minute and talk at 150. If in your meeting you are going through information (typically via a slide deck) which could equally well be read by those attending, you are going at one-third speed. Why not send out the information in advance and then use the meeting to agree the actions which come from it? If you are having the meeting in order to ensure that people know the information (i.e. to do the reading for them), you are allowing them to be lazy. Is it time for some tough love? If you didn't read it, you don't get to contribute. Deal with it.

Questions

- Which meetings do you need to push back on?

- How can you make the meetings you attend more productive?

- What will you do with the time you could save?

- Who else could help you to waste less time in meetings?

- When can you try out the INTRO model?

Make some notes on actions you need to take.

Tool 10. Know yourself

"The true value of a human being is determined primarily by the measure and sense in which he has obtained liberation from the self."

Albert Einstein

The clear gap in our team is for an extrovert completer-finisher spirit weasel... you can cover that Smithers

Introduction

When I look back on my life I realise how little I understood, let alone thought about, who I really am. My journey was initially mapped out for me by parents who felt I had potential as a

musician, and this had me from the age of eight travelling down a well-worn path: win a place in a cathedral choir, win a music scholarship to public school, win an organ scholarship to Oxford. Then I woke up momentarily to the realisation that I didn't want to make a career out of music, and some hasty applications to any large corporation that would have me, without any information about how corporate life would play to my strengths, or what type of work I would be best suited to. It was all guesswork.

I ended up getting a job offer from a large brewing and hospitality business, working in logistics. I immediately accepted it. And went on to waste 15 years fiddling about, trying to find something that flicked my switch. I never really did, apart from the last four years in marketing. Then they laid me off, so that was that.

Had I known and thought more about my strengths, I would do it very differently if I could do it all again.

This chapter is designed to get you thinking more carefully about your strengths and to what extent you are deploying them in your work. When I was in corporate land I was not achieving anything like my full potential, and I certainly did not have a well-functioning career mojo. That was avoidable: I could have made different career choices, negotiated a different emphasis within my role, developed myself more actively, and thus contributed more while being more fulfilled.

Which is exactly what Nina did when working for a tech company in Europe.

I was sitting in a conference room together with my manager and management team colleagues on a dreary morning back in the late 1990s. The management consultant who had facilitated our MBTI® test was revealing our team's many differences and similarities, but only one result stood out for me: I was diametrically opposed to my new manager. The two profile types on opposite ends of the flipchart diagram suddenly made everything fall into place – my feeling of not being understood or appreciated for my approach, and suddenly not being so happy in a job and company that I otherwise loved so much.

Prior to this exercise, I had sensed that my new manager and I had very different styles in everything from thinking and communicating to problem solving and managing people. I now realised I was trying to work with someone who only focused on the short term through micromanagement. I knew my motivation to do my best work was draining away and I had to make a change. Eventually I relocated and enjoyed a rewarding further 15 years in the organisation.

As you read this chapter, open your mind to the idea that you may not know yourself as well as you should, and this might be a missed opportunity for both you and your employer. Once you have found a way to know yourself better, do something with the information, just as Nina did. Try to treat is as more than an interesting intellectual exercise. It could make a crucial difference.

Play to your strengths

Knowing your strengths, building them and maximising their impact is a much more productive and fruitful way to develop yourself than it is to put energy into overcoming your weaknesses. This is the proposition Marcus Buckingham puts forward in his book *Now discover your strengths*.[55] The book includes a profile tool to help you identify what those strengths are, and as that is our topic in this chapter, I would recommend it to you.

This is such a liberating thought. He is saying that instead of trying to overcome my natural aversion to numbers and analysis thereof, I will reap better rewards in playing to my creative thinking and my ability to inspire others. Thank you very much, Marcus!

He doesn't suggest ignoring your weaknesses – recognise those, too, and develop them to the point where they don't inhibit you – but the rest is all about developing your strengths as a powerful resource.

How well do you know your strengths and how well are you able to deploy them in your role as it currently stands?

Creating room for your strengths

If you have answered those two questions and have recognised that your strengths aren't fully harnessed in your current role, what to do about it?

It could be that the only option is to find a new role. Section 3 of this book tackles that option in more detail. Let's assume for now that you're not ready to quit, but you would like things to change.

My suggestion is that you make a proposal for modifying your role so that you can play to your strengths more. If you do this in a way that results in a collaborative response, both parties stand to benefit. You become more productive and your mojo gets a boost. Research by the Corporate Leadership Council of nearly 20,000 employees shows that performance is between 21% and 36% higher in companies where managers emphasise strengths.[56] There are very sound business reasons alongside the well-being benefits of this approach.

As Caroline Webb puts it, when we are playing to our strengths and facing difficult challenges, "work might still feel tough, but it's easier for us to keep our brain in high-performance discovery mode when we're not constantly beset by a feeling that we're incompetent".[57] She goes on to report how research has shown that when volunteers found new ways to use their personal strengths, they reported higher levels of well-being, self-esteem and energy (what I would of course call a healthier career mojo).

This is about recognising the elements in your role that require you to deploy your weaker talents and proposing how else those requirements might be dealt with. Is there someone else who could do this work for whom it would be playing to their strengths? Could they be handled in a different way? Do they need to be done at all – could we do something else instead?

Assuming there is room for negotiation on those job components, what do you now have capacity to do which you didn't before, and how could that replacement activity play to your strengths?

Playing to your strengths doesn't, of course, necessarily require a renegotiation of your role. It may simply be a case of more mindfully playing to your strengths as you go about your job. You might find yourself using a new approach to the job and getting better results because you have more energy. You might also be more mindful when opportunities come up to work on projects or initiatives.

I remember when I worked in marketing I devised a loyalty programme for 4500 customers. It involved setting up a redemption catalogue so that customers could redeem their discount against merchandise to a value of what today would be more than £10 million per year. The strengths I deployed to get the scheme designed and approved were my creativity and communication skills. The trouble was that once the scheme went live it required a very different set of skills, principally in planning and detailed logistics organisation, neither of which are, shall we say, well developed in my strengths inventory. Fortunately, I was able to renegotiate my role so that someone else could take that on and do it to a far higher level of competence than I ever could, and I was able to put my energy into evolving the scheme and keeping it relevant.

Doing things that we are naturally drawn to and which motivate us does wonders for career mojo. There is a big difference between having a duty or obligation to do something and wanting to do something because we are naturally drawn to it. As Caroline Webb puts it: "When we get a chance to deploy our signature strengths, the research suggests we will feel especially energized and absorbed by whatever we're doing (almost by definition). And because this puts us so firmly in discovery mode, it enables higher performance, too."[58]

Know your team

I once organised a team offsite workshop for the consultants I used to manage. It was brilliantly facilitated by Anthony Landale, whom I knew from some breakthrough coaching he gave me when my career mojo was at a particularly low point.

He ran an exercise which I invite you to do for yourself as it was very powerful. He asked each of us to think of a particular moment when we were at our personal best: what he calls our "Best Self". What particular strengths were we using? How did it feel to be doing it this way? What was the impact on others?

Very simple, and very telling. As each of us shared our story we felt the team "glue" between us strengthen and we developed a real appreciation of each other's strengths. Someone talked about the run-up to their wedding. Another about the day his father died. I talked about something much more mundane: the day I and four other trainers flew to Cyprus to run five supposedly concurrent but identical management skills programmes, and when we got to the hotel discovered that they had only one large room for us, not five smaller ones. So we had to redesign the whole programme overnight (and sort out all the materials which had been soaked from being left on the airport tarmac in a downpour). We pulled it off and no one was any the wiser. We were exhausted but buzzing at the same time, liberated and energised by the creativity and teamwork between us.

Have a think about your Best Self story and tell someone else about it: your other team members, perhaps? What strengths were you accessing? How did it feel? What was the impact?

When a whole team knows their strengths, you can allocate work more intelligently. You can make up project teams so you have a good balance of strengths. You can use the information to recruit more intelligently as well, ensuring that you don't go and hire a new team member with a similar profile to everyone else, which is the natural tendency (because we like people who are like ourselves).

More insights into your preferences

In Tool 4 I talked about the Myers-Briggs® personality tool and how knowing your four-letter profile can help you in relationships with others. I just wanted to give you more personal insight into what the result can tell you. You can use this information in addition to your strengths profile to assess the type of work you do and better understand your responses to certain situations, some of which are no doubt positive and some of which may be negative.

Your four-letter profile gives you a clue as to how you respond to change. The table below shows how certain letter combinations indicate your response to change. Only one of these boxes has both letters in your four-letter profile.

Implications for change

IS Thoughtful Realist	IN Thoughtful Innovator
Concerned with practicalities. Likes to decide what to keep and what to change.	Concerned with thoughts, ideas concepts. Likes to generate new ideas and theories.
Learns by observing, reading, doing.	Learns by reading and listening.
"If it ain't broke, don't fix it."	**"Let's think ahead."**
ES Action Oriented Realist	**EN Action Oriented Innovator**
Concerned with ACTION! Likes to make things better.	Concerned with new ways of doing things. Likes to put new ideas into practice.
Learns by experimenting.	Learns creatively and with others.
"Let's just do it!"	**"If it ain't broke, break it!"**

ENs are life's change agents – constantly looking to innovate and improve, even if things are going well. The opposite are ISs, who like to protect what we already have and are less comfortable with change. ES and IN are somewhere in between.

Where do you sit? Are you at the IS end and working in an EN organisation or for an EN boss? If so, I imagine you find that quite stressful. Conversely, if you're more towards the EN mindset, you may get frustrated by others who don't respond to change as positively as you do. You might see them as slow or boring. How does that impact you and how might others perceive you?

This is a good place to remind you of what we covered in Tool 6, when I introduced the TKI Conflict model. Myers-Briggs® maps onto the Conflict Preferences model, with

Introverts preferring to Avoid, Extraverts to Collaborate, Thinkers to Compete and Feelers to Accommodate. Having this self-awareness and using it consciously can help you to play to your preferences.

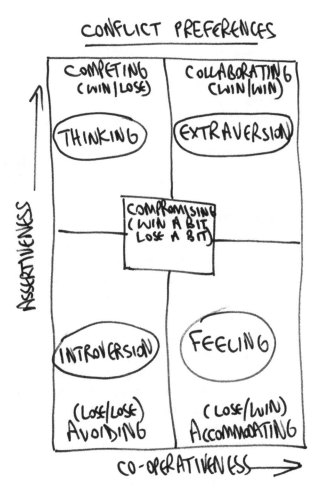

CONFLICT PREFERENCES

> I know, for instance, that I'm an Accommodator by choice. My work in the learning and development world involves me working with trainers and coaches who often have similar preferences, and as a rule we are helpful towards each other when we can be. I recognise that certain cultures where I find myself working have a very different approach to conflict.
>
> A large bank in New York springs to mind. I felt from the minute I met the client I was being judged, and I felt I would be spat out at the slightest sign of what they might detect as weakness: a very competitive culture, requiring me to up my assertiveness level, be less "fluffy" and more results driven. Tough Alpha-type language, strong eye contact, more formal attire and demeanour. I was well received there, but I was far from at ease, and there is no way their culture would have been a good fit for me.

A word about Introversion

Roughly half of us have a Myers-Briggs® preference for Introversion. Introverts get energy from inside themselves, through being quiet. They think deeply and in silence, stick with problems much longer than Extraverts do and tend to be less vocal in meetings.

The Western world tends to have a bias towards Extraversion. High levels of interaction with other people are encouraged – when you were young your parents probably told you to go out and play with the other kids rather than be in your bedroom playing with your trainset. The workplace tends to encourage people to meet and interact – nice noisy open-plan spaces so we can all see each other and bounce ideas around.

This is in effect a form of bullying. Introverts hate all that jazzed-up stuff. A noisy brainstorm is the least effective way to get ideas out of an Introvert. Far better to give them the problem to solve in advance of the meeting and let them come along having given it some thought.

If you are an Introvert, your working environment might be affecting your mojo. Interacting with others drains you. You can do it and come across as perfectly sociable; it's just that you prefer more peace and quiet and time to think. Consider whether there is some negotiation to do around your working environment – might you be more productive working from home more? Are there some options for working in a quieter part of the office when you need to do some deep thinking?

I suggest you have your team do the MBTI® so that you can compare profiles and learn more about how you might build better relationships between you based on this information.

The chameleon approach

This brings me to my final point in the chapter, and indeed in the 10-part mojo repair kit. Knowing yourself and understanding that others will have different preferences to yours is only a part of the story. Applying this information is where the emotional intelligence kicks in. You are not going to try to change the other person, but you are going to influence their response to you by adapting your own behaviour.

People like people who are like themselves. Putting yourself in their shoes, anticipating their concerns, giving them the level of detail they want, respecting their preference for Extraversion or Introversion: these are all changes you can make which will help you in connecting with and then influencing them.

The animal of choice for getting more of your own way, it seems to me, is the chameleon. Able to adapt to the context where necessary, to become the "colour" that matches the other person. This involves changes of mindset as well adapting our style, body language, voice, as we mentioned in Tool 4. The truth is, one size does not fit all. You just being you and expecting to influence across the whole range of personality types we've been discussing is not enough, I'm afraid. You need more options at your disposal if you want to influence some of the things we've been covering in this section of the book.

Summary

If as you've been reading the book you have decided to make some changes, you are going to need all the help you can get. The good news is that you don't need to look far for it because, to quote the Suede song, "It starts and ends with you". You are all you need to bring about the changes you have planned. Using your self-knowledge, you can think what you want to influence and how best to go about it.

Questions

- What personal strengths and preferences do you want to pay most attention to?

- What changes might you need to make in order for your strengths to be better harnessed?

- Where do you need to adapt your style and approach in order to build a better relationship?

- How do your strengths and preferences fit with the work you do?

Make some notes on actions you need to take.

Section 3
Replace the engine?

"There is a difference between giving up and giving in . . . there are many times when it is wise to give in, but never give up."

David McNally in Even eagles need a push[59]

Is your mojo beyond repair?

You only get one go on this beautiful little planet. Such a pity! How differently we might go about things if we could have a second pass at it.

I have met far too many people who recognise that their job isn't working and have run out of options. The only sensible course of action is to replace the engine: they need to start again, in whatever shape or form that might take. They know it, but they don't have the courage or, they tell themselves, the opportunity to do anything about it.

This chapter is designed to give those people a prod on the arm. Maybe they have lost sight of what's important or are allowing some faulty thinking to prevent them from making the first move. This has to come from you – sitting around waiting for your boss to help you leave is unlikely to happen, let's be honest. Assuming you're functioning at a reasonable level of competence, your departure would create a headache involving time, risk, cost and productivity impact which they could well do without, thank you very much. You can expect the same unspoken concerns from your employer, one of whose primary aims is to reduce employee churn rate and employment costs as well as retaining the good people in an increasingly competitive market.

So this is one where Stephen Covey's "be proactive"[60] habit is needed more than ever. You have to make the first move. Sorry about that. Tough love.

Warning lights

Let's look at the dashboard and see what warning lights have come on. If any of these are showing red, I'd suggest you stop driving immediately.

Misalignment of values

If your values do not fit with another's, you are inherently in a conflict situation. I experienced this at various stages of my career and it was debilitating. The misalignment may be with the organisation's cultural values, or it might be with an individual (probably your boss). They say people don't leave their company, they leave their boss. That was my experience.

I met Guy Arnold many years ago when we were both new to the hospitality business. He shared his experience of a misalignment of values which led to him leaving his organisation.

"In an internal interview for a promotion, I was asked by my boss for my thoughts on how we, as a UK pub company, could grow the business in what had been a fairly stagnant market.

"I replied that the clear growth area was in the area of eating out. We should offer our support and evolve our business approach to ensure that our customers (tenants who were obliged to buy their drinks from us) could run busier and more profitable businesses based on building successful catering operations.

The reply I received shocked me in both its aggression and its scarcity mindset: 'There's no bloody legal tie on food, we make no profit from it, so there's no way we're going to waste our time and effort supporting it.'

"I got the job (despite this radical difference in views) but ended up regretting it as we always seemed to be on the back foot, struggling with ever increasing instability in the estate, stagnant rents and falling beer sales (and with the above mindset still firmly in place). This conflict never went away, of course, and after a few long and miserable years I left the business."

What is the "Why?"

In the first chapter of Section 2 – Tool 1 (Reset your compass) – I got you thinking about Simon Sinek's Golden Circle[61] and considering your own "Why" as well as that for your team and indeed your organisation.

If there is a major mis-fit between your "Why" and that of the organisation, you might conclude that this is beyond fixing. I can think of lots of examples where this has been the case and the result has been people leaving. In one instance the individual's "Why" was to help other people to achieve their full potential through learning. He felt that his employer's "Why" was to maximise profits in readiness for selling the business prior to retirement. After two stressful and unfulfilling years, he left.

In the UK this is happening on a macro level within the National Health Service, where many doctors are showing increasing dissatisfaction with the way politicians are driving the service. A survey published in the *British Medical Journal* in August 2017 of more than 2000 doctors in South West England revealed that 70% reported a career intention which would negatively impact GP capacity over the next five years. In other words, they planned to leave, reduce their hours or take a career break. The report concluded: "There is thus an urgent need to find ways of retaining the GP workforce. If unaddressed, 'meltdown' in NHS care may follow within the foreseeable future."[62]

You may also have concluded that your organisation does not have a "Why" and that in itself might lead you to being unclear about how you can align with it. I remember a conversation with a mid-career manager in customer services in the technology industry. "I find myself asking why I am driving what seems like every hour of every day towards something which will ultimately enhance the customer invoicing experience. It's like, what's the point?" She now works with a charity supporting young people, mojo very much back in operation.

How's your boss?

Your boss has such a powerful influence on your well-being. I've had both good and bad. I've told you more than enough about Boss from Hell earlier in the book. My best bosses have recognised my strengths and let me play to them, giving me maximum room to be creative and drive my own agenda, with just light-touch management when necessary. That style worked really well for me and I was able to contribute successfully. The difference between how I felt getting up in the morning with Boss from Hell versus the light-touch liberating style was the difference between night and day.

I hear stories from people who have a "virtual" boss based in a different region (and often time zone), whom they have never actually met. What does this say about the boss' priorities?

Insecure bosses are often those who have been promoted because they were good technically at their job, not because they are good people managers. This is not their fault, they just haven't had the support or been given the time to learn how to manage people effectively, so they default to hands-on micromanagement, to the detriment of both parties.

There are bosses who "just don't get it". Research shows that the biggest barrier potentially to implementing what you learn on a training course is your line manager. "Get back into line," they say when you try out a new approach, because they themselves haven't learned those skills. Is your boss like that, and is that something you can live with?

Are you avoiding?

If in your heart of hearts you recognise that it really is time to replace the engine, I urge you to avoid avoidance, as I said in Tool 6. Conflict grows the longer you leave it, and if you avoid it, it may become harder to make the move – you will add to the agony by having it on your mind for longer and feeling guilty that you are avoiding, and meanwhile the clock is ticking, you're not getting any younger and there may be a huge upside you are missing out on.

It's really easy to list reasons not to make this difficult move. Here are some of the regular ones I hear:

- I have a mortgage to pay so I can't take the financial risk.
- I'll be letting other people down.
- I don't know how to run my own business.
- I'm too old to get another job.
- My skills aren't relevant enough.
- I am too expensive.

You might like to write down your list of Reasons To Not Quit My Job. Then show it to someone you trust and between you ask yourselves:

- Am I exaggerating?
- Am I assuming?
- Is this logical?

You may discover that you are telling yourself things that don't stand up well to scrutiny.

What's the upside?

Make another list: all the reasons and benefits you can think of to quit your job. Someone else might be able to do this one as sometimes you stop yourself from seeing the upside.

Now compare the two lists. What's the net result? How important and life-changing are the items on the second list and to what extent do they offset the concerns on the first?

You may be surprised by the results.

Getting started

"A journey of a thousand miles begins with a single step." So said Chinese philosopher Lao Tzu. I'm a great believer in this and it applies in so many areas of life – for instance, when teaching someone to play the piano. When they find a passage difficult, we play with one hand at a time, really slowly, bar by bar, until it becomes fluent. Then we play with both hands slowly and gradually build up the speed. Eventually it is fluent and totally comfortable.

When you're making major life changes, identifying the *first step* and writing it down is the best way to get started. I remember being coached many years back and being asked to write down the five things I wanted to achieve over the next two years. I wrote down:

- Change my job.
- Move house.
- Sort out my finances.
- Plan how to fund the children's education.
- Get my left eye sorted out.

I was then asked to write down the first step for each of these. I still have the piece of paper because it was such a watershed and truly life-changing moment for me. It looks like this:

Change my job	Discuss options with boss	Next week
Move house	Get estate agent to value our house	Next week
Sort out my finances	Get mortgage redemption quote	Tomorrow
Plan the kids' education	Request 5 school brochures	Next week
Get my eye sorted out	Make doctor's appointment	Tomorrow

Within two years I had changed job, sold our house and moved 200 miles away (thus redeeming our mortgage in the process), got my children lined up for private education and had a cataract removed in my left eye. Life-changing, and a great set of boosts to my career mojo.

But all of these started with one small and not scary-looking first step. Then, of course, things build their own momentum and you may end up wondering why you took so long to get round to it.

I urge you to write down the plan and keep it visible, and share it with someone close to you.

Summary

When I look back I recognise that I dithered and faffed around at various moments in my far-from-illustrious career. That was never at any point a good thing, and I wasted too many good years working with a slightly bad taste in my mouth. I could have achieved so much more. It has only been in the last 10 years, since I went self-employed, that I feel I have really started to find genuine fulfilment. And this last year when I started to write this book I have discovered something else about myself which I plan to draw on more, which is how easy I find it to write and how satisfying it is. So that is another chapter I need to start for myself as I continue to strive after my full potential.

Let's finish with one more quote, which resonates so well for me:

"Many men go fishing all of their lives without knowing it is not fish they are after."

Henry Thoreau

Questions

- What have you decided?

- What are the benefits?

- Who can help you?

- What do you need to do first?

Make some notes on the first steps you are going to take and share them with someone close. Keep them visible.

Section 4
Mojo maintenance

"Give me a lever long enough... and single-handed I can move the world."

Archimedes

Introduction

Even a well-tuned engine needs maintenance. It needs oil, fuel and regular good practice in order to keep it in peak condition.

This chapter is designed to have you review how well you maintain your mojo and to suggest one or two adjustments you might make to tune it up a little.

Stimulation levels

There is an optimum level of stimulation in our lives that produces maximum energy and sense of well-being – what I've called career mojo, as you know. Your optimum stimulation level will be different to mine and will depend on such things as the stage you're at in your life, whether you prefer Introversion or Extraversion, and so on.

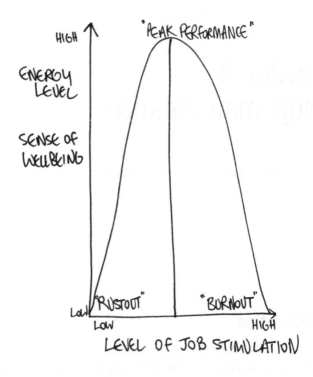

Where are you on this diagram? What are the sources of stimulation or stress in your life and how can you optimise this? What do you want more of and what do you want less of?

Have a think about what aspects of your life take the most energy and the least energy.

What gives you the most energy and how could you get more of it?

Are there aspects of your life where you should stop fighting your corner and just go with the flow?

Some popular mojo blockers

These are some of the most popular mojo blockers I come across with mid-careerers. Put a tick against the ones you like.

- ☐ Working too hard
- ☐ Not sharing
- ☐ Doing things that aren't important
- ☐ Never taking time to reflect and learn
- ☐ Doing everything perfectly
- ☐ Being obsessed by deadlines
- ☐ Not negotiating
- ☐ Not knowing what's required
- ☐ Doing things that are no longer relevant or required
- ☐ Never saying "no"
- ☐ Not securing the resources needed
- ☐ Not being clear on who does what
- ☐ Making assumptions
- ☐ Keeping the customer at arm's length
- ☐ Jumping in too fast
- ☐ Not asking enough questions
- ☐ Being too available
- ☐ Being obsessed with social media.
- ☐ Add your own................................

Which ones do you need to work on?

Adjust your mindset

Your attitude towards any situation is a choice. You choose whether to be angry (usually when you do, you won't get what you want) or to collaborate. You choose whether to have a scarcity or an abundance mentality. You choose to make something a point of principle or to let it go.

I have found that yourself, with all your vulnerabilities and anxieties, is the best person to be. Trying to fake it and make out you are someone else is not only hard to sustain, it's also rarely a total success – people see through it and then you come across as insincere or inconsistent and they won't trust you. And, worst of all, it's tiring. A great way to suck out your energy is to go around with a fake persona. Yes, there's a time and a place to be someone else, for the purposes of the moment – that meeting with the CEO, that make-or-break client presentation you have to deliver. But not all the time.

If you can bring some humour and some humility to the situation, you will find it reduces defend-and attack responses from others. It builds a discovery mindset, which is good for all involved. And guess what – it makes life more fun. We don't have to wear serious faces all day long, do we? Surely life is too short not to be allowed to enjoy our work. That little dopamine rush from the amusing personal anecdote is a shot in the arm for us all.

Maintenance tips

When I was carrying out research into what specifically mid-careerers are most worried about, one of the biggest concerns which came out was how to remain relevant: having the right skill set and being up to speed with how the world is evolving.

This is an understandable concern. I recently listened to John Kern, Senior Vice President of Cisco's Supply Chain Operations, speaking at the company's Supply Chain University Development Day.

"You have to keep up your pace of learning or run the risk of becoming obsolete. We have to keep pushing

ourselves to remain relevant, and to do that you have to figure out ways to learn."

One of the skills he alluded to was being able to assess how the work you do makes an impact on the business.

"Otherwise you're not going to be as effective as you could be and it's not going to be as rewarding."

It makes sense to do that by keeping in touch with the younger generation who are driving so much of the social change around us. Get social, as they say. John Doerr is a venture capitalist in Forbes' Top 100 list of greatest living business minds. This is how he does it:

"Here's how I stay relevant. I read. I listen. I try to surround myself with smart people of all ages and backgrounds."

Do you need to actively network with a younger age group in order to learn new skills and see how they cope with today's demands? Doerr says he reads. Voraciously, I wouldn't mind betting. When I was doing my research I asked people specifically how often they read and was surprised at how many of them rarely do, and if so it is in a very limited field. I set myself a goal of reading at least 20 business books a year and aim to supplement that with biography and fiction in order to broaden my mind and keep my brain functioning. It's hardly surprising if people feel they are slipping out of touch if the only things they read are news digests on their phones.

But here's a worrying thought: Are we all losing the ability to read? I find myself totally recognising what author Michael Harris says in this article titled "I have forgotten how to read".[63]

"Turning, one evening, from my phone to a book, I set myself the task of reading a single chapter in one sitting. Simple. But I couldn't. There was nothing wrong with

my eyes. No stroke or disease clouded my way. Yet – if I'm being honest – the failure was also not a surprise.

Paragraphs swirled; sentences snapped like twigs; and sentiments bled out. The usual, these days. I drag my vision across the page and process little. Half an hour later, I throw down the book and watch some Netflix.

Out for dinner with another writer, I said, 'I think I've forgotten how to read.'

'Yes!' he replied, pointing his knife. 'Everybody has.'

'No, really,' I said. 'I mean I actually can't do it anymore.'

He nodded: 'Nobody can read like they used to. But nobody wants to talk about it.'

For good reason. It's embarrassing. Especially for someone like me. I'm supposed to be an author – words are kind of my job. Without reading, I'm not sure who I am. So, it's been unnerving to realize: I have forgotten how to read – really read – and I've been refusing to talk about it out of pride.

But online life makes me into a different kind of reader – a cynical one. I scrounge, now, for the useful fact; I zero in on the shareable link. My attention – and thus my experience – fractures. Online reading is about clicks, and comments, and points. When I take that mindset and try to apply it to a beaten-up paperback, my mind bucks.

Even Eric Schmidt, the erstwhile chief executive of Google, was anxious about the mental landscape he was helping to cultivate. He once told Charlie Rose: 'I worry that the level of interrupt, the sort of overwhelming rapidity of information ... is in fact affecting cognition. It is affecting deeper thinking. I still believe that sitting down and reading a book is the best way to really learn something. And I worry that we're losing that.' In fact, there's a great deal of reporting now – from neuroscientists such as Susan Greenfield and Gary Small – to show that digital native brains do engage in concretely different ways from those of previous generations. Spend 10 hours a day staring at screens and – yes – your synapses will adapt.

For a long time, I convinced myself that a childhood spent immersed in old-fashioned books would insulate me somehow from our new media climate – that I could keep on reading and writing in the old way because my mind was formed in pre-internet days. But the mind is plastic – and I have changed. I'm not the reader I was."

Harris goes on to say that if the way we read has changed, that will change the way we write. And if that happens – what he forecasts to be a more cynical way of writing – then we are losing something fundamental to our society as human beings. They have taken spelling off the school curriculum in Finland, presumably because predictive text makes it no longer necessary. What next – writing? Arithmetic? Where does that all lead us? Back to the caves, I imagine.

It's not the aim of this book to tell you how to keep fit or change your diet to maintain yourself physically. I'm just grateful that walking the dog twice a day is, my friend Dr Will Liddell tells me, a very good way to take exercise – regularly and not putting too much strain on the body. Eat your greens and lots of yogurt and don't drink too much. There's my expert input, for what it's worth.

I would just ask you whether you're getting enough sleep. I recently read an article by Matthew Walker, who has been studying how sleep affects the human mind and body for two decades. He concludes that we're in the midst of a "catastrophic sleep loss epidemic", the consequences of which are far graver than you can imagine. He has discovered powerful links between sleep loss and Alzheimer's, cancer, diabetes, obesity and anxiety. Apparently nearly 50% of us are trying to get by on less than six hours of sleep per night. Longer commutes, free access to alcohol and caffeine and higher levels of anxiety are part of the story, of course.[64]

"We've stigmatised sleep with the label of laziness. We want to seem busy, and one way we express that is by proclaiming how little sleep we're getting."

Walker has a non-negotiable eight hours every night. There are sound medical reasons for this:

"After just one night of only four or five hours' sleep, your natural killer cells – the ones that attack the cancer cells that appear in your body every day – drop by 70%."

In the workplace, lack of sleep has been shown to amplify the reaction of the amygdala – a key part of the brain responsible for triggering anger and rage – by 60%. If you find yourself having emotional outbursts at work, lack of sleep could be the culprit. Is a change of sleep routine something you need to consider?

What type of people do you surround yourself with? Do they give you energy or sap it? How actively are you building your professional network so that you are receiving a regular feed of what's hot and what's not?

Get yourself a mentor or a coach. Someone who has either trodden the same path as you (mentor) or a coach to help you tread your own path. Just having the support and interest of someone independent and objective can be a great boost and a source of well-being.

It's all too easy to slip into comfortable habits and lose sight of the need to constantly work out our mojo. It really is up to you whether you choose to be proactive or whether you prefer seeing what shows up.

Questions

- What routines do you want to include to help nurture your mojo?

- What might you want to stop doing?

- Who can help you?

- When do you start?

Make a maintenance plan, write it down and share it with someone close. Keep it visible.

Summary

Keeping this alive

When I wrote this book my intention was to help people who might be struggling to find their way in an increasingly challenging workplace. If you have found just one suggestion here that you feel able to apply and that makes a difference, I will have achieved what I set out to do. I hope it's more than that, of course, but even if it is just one and it works, I'll be happy.

Often we get to the end of a three-day training course and people start to display anxiety. "I'm excited and I'm worried," they say. Worried about how they are going to keep the learning alive once they get back to the pressures of the workplace.

You may have the same anxiety, which I totally understand. So here are some suggestions that might help.

Firstly, remember that you are in many cases going to try to change your habits. This will require regular conscious changes which eventually (thankfully) you will not need to remember any more. In the early stage you will need to consciously practise. Your brain requires far less energy to run on autopilot and given a choice it will always seek out the easy path. So this is going to require effort and may be tiring.

Reward, Remind, Repeat

Caroline Webb has some excellent advice on how to make these new approaches stick. She suggests the Reward, Remind, Repeat mantra.[65]

Reward: when you score a success through trying out one of my suggestions, it is natural to not spend any time analysing what was successful and how you can repeat it. However, neuroscientists, psychologists and economists tell us that the brain will naturally seek out rewards where it can, so if you reward yourself with a mental pat on the back and a moment to reflect on what went well, you are more likely to repeat the behaviour.

You can of course do something more obvious, such as giving yourself another biscuit or going home early that night.

Remind: find yourself whatever visual or tactile prompt works best for you, so that the behaviour you are trying to change is prompted in some way by it. I have heard of people who have a little visual reminder on the whiteboard in their office or on their desk. Screensavers. A photo of the model or excerpt from a book on their phone. Or an object: a talisman of some sort in your pocket. A photo. A piece of art.

On one of the leadership programmes I run I give people a book to take away and I write a personal message in the front. Someone showed me a photo of the page on her phone the other day and said when she is stressed she refers to it to remind her of the bigger picture.

I have to work hard at not talking too fast when I present, and one way I do that is by printing out the slides nine per page, and writing SLOW DOWN or PAUSE at least once per page. It works for me.

You can also ask a colleague for feedback on the behaviour you're working on, to see whether you are applying it and what the impact is. Nothing like being held accountable by someone else to motivate you to make the change.

Repeat: I mentioned at the start of the book that "neurons that fire together, wire together". As they do so, the behaviour becomes more and more natural, to the point that you will eventually not need to consciously access it. Think back to when you learned how to tie your shoelaces. You no longer have to think about it, but at the time it was a slow and clumsy process, which didn't always go smoothly. That's perfectly fine and is to be expected. When you try out these new behaviours, attitudes and beliefs, they may feel clumsy and unnatural because you may be breaking some old habits which have formed over years.

So embrace that feeling of discomfort: if it feels weird, it's because you are doing something differently. That awkward sensation is a clue that you are trying out something new and for that you should give yourself an internal round of applause.

Other tips for creating habits

- Set yourself a reminder in your Calendar app in three months' time. The reminder might be the specific item, or it might be a prompt to read again a certain section of this book or one of the resources I have pointed out.

- Get coached on the behaviour you want to change. A good coach will help you to think things through and ask you some pertinent questions which will help you to work out what you need to do. The coach might also be able to offer advice if that is appropriate, or challenge you if you're making assumptions. It's also useful to simply talk things out and to hear yourself articulate what is going on inside your head.

- Coach someone else. There is nothing quite like coaching someone else in order to learn yourself. Coaching someone else requires you to organise your own thoughts and to find words to describe what is going on inside your brain. You don't have to be expert on the topic, and both you and the person you're coaching will get great value from the dialogue.

- Give yourself a deadline. Some of your actions may involve doing something you have avoided up until now. Setting a deadline for it will give you a focus and may help you to avoid letting it drift. Set yourself a reminder in your Calendar and be hard on yourself if you let it slip. This is self-management, and you need to be your toughest critic!

Further help

If you have found the ideas in this book useful and want to explore them further, one way to do that could be to work on them with a group of like-minded people. For that reason I have developed a two-day workshop which is based on the 10 tools we have covered in the book. It is open to anyone from any organisation, so if you attend, the chances are you will meet people with similar challenges to you but from a different organisation or market sector.

Details of workshops are available on my website: www.myjobisntworking.com

What we haven't covered

Of course, this book hasn't been the whole story. I haven't attempted to address other areas which might be affecting your career mojo, such as internal politics, dealing with hidden agendas, business strategy, workplace processes and procedures and so on. Not my field, and there are plenty of other books out there to help with that.

Final thoughts

If the aim of the book has been to spread a little more human happiness and make a difference to people's experience of life, can I urge you to do the same for others? There's nothing like coaching someone in order to develop your own skills, so it's another great way to reinforce the changes you want to make.

But may I also ask you to do what you can to build the humanity around the place? Be a little bit more kind. Be more generous with your time. Give people the benefit of the doubt – maybe they are a good person, just in a bad situation. Find more time to connect as humans and to work more closely together as individuals – just like we used to years ago, if you're old enough to remember.

One last request

Whatever you decide to do now, please do something! Don't just put this book away and forget about it. I feel passionately about this, and here's why.

My friend Will Liddell has worked for the National Health Service as a doctor for nearly 30 years. When he and I were discussing this book he told me what it's like to work in a doctor's surgery day after day.

"I meet a constant stream of people who are coming to me because they feel unwell and where it is quickly obvious that this is work-related. They are hoping that there is a medical explanation for their condition and that I can prescribe some form of medication.

Regrettably, I can't. They don't need to see me, they need a coach or some other form of help.

"What is particularly worrying is that they appear not to have realised that their stress at work is affecting their health or mental well-being. It has somehow crept up on them, and by the time they come and see me, the problem has become acute. While not too late to remedy, they have endured so much avoidable misery and I wish I could do more. Sadly, this really is a case where the only person who can help them is themselves."

Resources

I have tried to include details of all my sources. If I have unintentionally missed out something or you can fill in a gap for me, please let me know and we'll include it in the next edition.

Date and publisher information provided is the current version on Amazon.co.uk. It can vary from original date of publication.

Acknowledgements

I have so many people I want to thank. Where shall I start? Why not at the beginning?

Dr Will Liddell is an old school friend, and we meet up a couple of times every year to compare notes and reminisce. Eighteen months ago he said to me, "We should write a book together." He planted a seed which has become this book. (We didn't write it together because he had too many other fish to fry last year. The idea hasn't gone away though. Watch this space.)

Having decided I wanted to write this book, I turned to my network for ideas on how to go about it. My first thought was to contact Penny Pullan, who co-wrote her book *Business Analysis & Leadership* a few years ago and invited me to contribute a chapter. She put me straight on to Alison Jones, who regularly runs an extraordinary event called "The 10-day business book proposal challenge" on Facebook. I signed up and 10 days later had a full publisher proposal ready to go. Thank you, Alison, for being there right from the start and, as it turned out, right through to the end (I eventually decided to work with Alison to publish the book).

Once I'd "graduated" Alison's group I knew how much the support of peers who are also writing a business book meant to me. So I joined a Business Book Mastermind group also run by Alison, where I got to know Jude Jennison, Elaine Halligan and Anne Archer very well. Their support and encouragement as well as their great suggestions for the book were invaluable, and I doubt I would have written it had it not been for them.

I knew I had the material for the book inside my head, but felt a need to validate my thinking with some hard research. So I reached out to my database of contacts who, in the main, I had worked with in a training environment over the years. Some 150 contributed to that research, giving me some hard data and the confidence to press on with the project. I'm grateful to each and every one of you:

John Gough, Matthew Fangman, Malcolm Forbes-Cable, John Savic, Vikas Vats, Rie Norum, Chen Wang, Oscar Salvidar, Lee Hudson, Kathy Mendoza, Chintan Sheth, Nina Heldt, Dandy Franz, Simarjeet Kaur, Heidi Yin, Rob Bell, Kikki Singh, Richard Ho, Elena Rodstein, Jim Arnold, Karen Hill, Jorge Rodriguez, Anirban Guha, Mamatha Prasad, Abbey Burns, Sonia van der Linden Pugal, Angela Kao, Abu Asim, Natalia Novikova, Alan Sung, Thiery Boonen, Ian Threadgold, Jenny Large, Ben Holt, Katarina Kovacevic, Sheila Robertson, Thomas Hallstein, Mary Moore, Alejandro Fernandez, Brian Balistreri, Peter Vansa, Mike Morrisson, Wale Owoeye, Marcus Gallo, Aakriti Dharmani, Steve Sinos, Kevin McDonnell, Gonzalo Martin-Villa Pena, Mark Cockerton, Earl Talbot, Riccardo Bua, Pradeep Jadhav, Florian Otto, Beryl Cuckney, Amanda Jenkins, Veronica Recanati, Gill Bardinet, Jamie Cole, Chelsea Robertson, David Christie, Frazer Thompson, Tushar Bansal, Ken Thomas, Romonda Goodwin, Jane Ansell, Victor Newman, Shanita Woodward, Howard Langley, Jonathan Graham, Tracey Hooper, Gary Westfal, Liat Shenster, Damian Goodburn, Wim Symoen, Morag Mathieson, Rupert Trevelyan, David Auty, Teresa Fernandez, Yaroslav Krasnov, Torbjorn Soltvedt, Vanessa Clarke, Manuela Burg, Ceej Morley, Bob Hawken, David Thomas, Usman Majeed.

Ian Small and I spent many hours together in training rooms around the world rolling out a leadership programme for which he was the sponsor. He struck me then as one of the most impressive leaders I have ever met, not least through the sheer investment of his time as COO of a large division within a huge company attending each and every one of the iterations of the programme. He walked the talk of the programme, memorably on certain occasions diving in and sharing his stories and experiences. When I asked him to write the foreword, I had my fingers very firmly crossed, as I knew that if he agreed he would write something from the heart and give it 100% of his attention. Which of course he did. I am honoured and eternally grateful, Ian.

I set up a group of beta readers to give me feedback along the way. Thank you all for your forthright (James, you excelled yourself at this!) and supportive feedback:

James Roberston, Xue Peng, Sara Bailey, James Seed, Vinita Temmert, Tom Cooper, Mark Woodhead, Howard Ellison, Mandy Green, Spencer Holmes, Ian Walker, Guy Arnold, Kim Autry, Emma Brown, Yaroslav Krasnov.

More than 250 people joined my "launch team" and helped us to get the word out right from the day of publication. Thank you all for your enthusiasm and support:

I am amazed to have received the endorsements I have, and am honoured to be able to have printed them. They mean so much. Thank you Ralph Kilmann, Marshall Goldsmith, Kevan Hall, Rob Goffee, Peter Vicary-Smith, Nina Gullerud, Ian Walker, Petra Merne, Ray Bremner, Guy Arnold.

Thank you Will Liddell for the cartoons. What a great excuse to muck about together again!

To Alison's publishing team, my eternal thanks. You were so nice to this newbie.

Thank you Nancy Kline, Leatta Haugh for giving me permission to use your material.

I wanted to use this moment to thank my children, Emma and James, for putting up with a Dad who was all too often not around when he should have been. A trainer's life is an inherently antisocial one, in that pretty much every day in a training room involves getting to the venue the night before (and of course thus being away from home for the night). In my case all too often that was via an international flight. Sunday afternoons were regularly ruined by Dad having to head off, usually stressed by the thought of arriving at the airport too late and therefore not in the best of spirits. I mucked it up for all of us, yet I don't remember either of you ever complaining. Thank you.

And so finally to my wife, Charlotte, without whom none of this would have been possible. You have kept it all together for us, and provided the steady and totally reliable base from which I have been able to conduct my unpredictable forays into uncharted waters week in week out, for nearly 20 years. You're amazing. You are my rock.

I want to let her have the last word. One of the best bits of feedback I ever received from anyone was over the breakfast table one morning, when as usual I wasn't listening. She leaned over and said the immortal words which are now my mantra:

"Sit up, shut up and listen up!"

THE END

(Or is it in fact the beginning?)

Epilogue

I never thought I would find myself writing these extraordinary words.

On Easter Saturday, I woke up and found my wife Charlotte, to whom I was married for 36 years, lying dead beside me. She had suffered a pulmonary embolism: a massive clot in the pulmonary artery, causing painless but instant death. Neither she nor I knew anything about it. She was a fit and healthy 57 year old: a dog-walking non-smoker on no medication who didn't know the name of her doctor because she never needed to meet him.

Initially I was tempted to rewrite much of the book based on this life-changing experience, but I then realised it is more powerful to leave it completely unchanged (and this includes the last paragraph on the previous page). The messages in the book seem to me to support the two huge learning points which have come out of this:

1. Take *nothing* for granted, especially the important things. If this can sneak up on someone as healthy as Charlotte, it can happen to anyone. Repeat: Anyone.

   Please, please recognise what is important and cherish it.

2. Make every day count. You will never know how long you have on this lovely planet. Why would you waste it vegging out in front of the TV, checking your Facebook

likes, doing work that adds no value, chugging along in the middle lane, when you could be doing so much more? Don't let it slip through your fingers. You *can* make a difference with your special gifts, so what are you waiting for?

In order for Charlotte's death to have meaning I am going to raise £50,000 for the British Heart Foundation to help it research and combat heart disease. I will be donating all my proceeds from the sale of this book to specifically support the £35 million thrombosis research programme the Foundation is doing at Birmingham University. The research team has already identified a way to screen blood for a propensity for veins to constrict and this could lead to a major impact on the number of unexpected cardiovascular deaths worldwide.

If through our fundraising we make it more likely that just one person does not die before their time, Charlotte's passing will not have been without meaning.

I have set up a Just Giving page to support the fundraising. If you feel this book has helped you and you would like to recognise this by supporting the research, here's the link: www.justgiving.com/fundraising/charliebrownchagford   By buying the book you have already contributed, for which I am extremely grateful.

As you can see, I intend to get through this, principally by applying an approach much espoused by Churchill, which at one (fleeting) point was going to be the title for this book: *KBO: Keep Buggering On.*

This book now has a renewed purpose, and it motivates me like crazy.

My love to you all.

> *"An ending is just a beginning in disguise."*

Researching deep vein thrombosis (DVT)

The processes that cause DVT are still not understood. Thanks to funding from the British Heart Foundation, researchers around the country are working to change that.

They are exploring how small cells in the blood (platelets) are activated, how this may lead to DVT and ways to prevent activation without causing bleeding. They have identified a protein on the surface of the platelet, CLEC-2, which is involved in this. They are also testing a drug that is already used for another condition, which could be used to block platelet activation. This will speed up the process to help save lives.

This is only one aspect of this devastating condition that is being researched. To develop a thorough understanding of DVT and help prevent premature death because of it, researchers are also formulating an innovative model in which to examine the influence of platelet–neutrophil interactions in the initiation and development of DVT. The blood contains many cell types, including platelets (involved in blood clotting) and white blood cells (neutrophils) that are part of our immune system. These two cell types can interact in several ways. The research teams have discovered a novel way in which these cells can bind to each other, which may be particularly important in investigating the development and severity of DVT.

This is an exciting area of research for humanity, which will widen our knowledge and understanding of the trigger that initiates DVT and thus will lead to prevention and a lowering of the number of premature deaths caused by DVT.

Endnotes

1. Gallup, "State of the American workplace survey" Gallup. com (2017) http://news.gallup.com/businessjournal/203957/ american-workplace-changing-dizzying-pace.aspx (accessed February 2018).

2. Gallup, "State of the global workplace report" Gallup.com (2017) www.gallup.com/services/178517/state-global-workplace.aspx (accessed February 2018).

3. Jennifer Grasz, "CareerBuilder study reveals top ten productivity killers at work" CareerBuilder.com (2014) www.careerbuilder.com/share/aboutus/pressreleasesdetail. aspx?ed=12/31/2014&id=pr827&sd=6/12/2014 (accessed February 2018).

4. Stephen Covey, The 7 habits of highly effective people (2004).

5. Dov Seidman, How: why how we do anything means everything (2011).

6. Michael LeGault, Think: why crucial decisions can't be made in the blink of an eye (2006).

7. Thomas Friedman, Thank you for being late (2016), chapter 2.

8. Stephen MR Covey, The speed of trust (2006).

9. Thomas Friedman, Thank you for being late (2017).

10. Michael Chui, James Manyika and Nehdi Miremadi, "Where machines could replace humans – and where they can't (yet)" in McKinsey Quarterly, July (2016) www.mckinsey.com/business-functions/digital-mckinsey/our-insights/where-machines-could-

replace-humans-and-where-they-cant-yet (accessed February 2018).

[11] Larry Elliott, "Robots threaten 15m UK jobs, says Bank of England's Chief Economist" at Guardian online (12 November 2015) www.theguardian.com/business/2015/nov/12/robots-threaten-low-paid-jobs-says-bank-of-england-chief-economist (accessed February 2018).

[12] Thomas Friedman, Thank you for being late (2016), chapter 5.

[13] Ibid, chapter 8.

[14] Adair Turner "The real demographic challenge" at Project-syndicate.org (21 August 2015) www.project-syndicate.org/commentary/demographic-challenge-poor-countries-by-adair-turner-2015-08?barrier=accessreg (accessed February 2018).

[15] Stephen Hawking "This is the most dangerous time for our planet" at theguardian.com (1 December 2016) www.theguardian.com/commentisfree/2016/dec/01/stephen-hawking-dangerous-time-planet-inequality (accessed February 2018).

[16] Rolf Dobelli, The art of the good life (2017).

[17] Wolfgang Bock, Dominic Field, Paul Zwillenberg and Kristi Rogers "The growth of the global mobile internet economy" at BCG.com (February 2015) www.bcg.com/en-ca/publications/2015/technology-industries-growth-global-mobile-internet-economy.aspx (accessed February 2018).

[18] Will Dahlgreen, "37% of British workers think their jobs are meaningless" at Yougov.co.uk (August 2015) https://yougov.co.uk/news/2015/08/12/british-jobs-meaningless/ (accessed February 2018).

[19] Gallup, "State of the American workplace survey" at Gallup.com (2017) http://news.gallup.com/businessjournal/203957/american-workplace-changing-dizzying-pace.aspx (accessed February 2018).

[20] Ken Thomas, Intrinsic motivation at work (2009).

[21] Simon Sinek, Start with why (2011).

22 Victor Frankl, Man's search for meaning (2004) published by Rider. Reproduced by permission of The Random House Group Ltd.

23 Nadine Stair (attr.), "If I had my life to live over" based on the text "I'd pick more daisies" by Don Herold (pre-1935).

24 Denise Rousseau, Psychological contract in organizations: understanding written and unwritten agreements (1995).

25 Department of Economics, University of Sheffield, "Workplace trust key factor in productivity" at Sheffield ac.uk (21 August 2015) www.sheffield.ac.uk/faculty/social-sciences/news/workplace-trust-1.499084 (accessed February 2018).

26 20th CEO survey, section 3 "Gaining connectivity without losing trust" at Pwc.com (2017) www.pwc.com/gx/en/ceo-survey/2017/pwc-ceo-20th-survey-report-2017.pdf (accessed February 2017).

27 Edelman Trust Barometer – UK findings at Edelman.com (2017) www.edelman.co.uk/magazine/posts/edelman-trust-barometer-2017-uk-findings/ (accessed February 2018).

28 2018 Edelman Trust Barometer at Edelman.com (2018) www.edelman.com/trust-barometer (accessed February 2018).

29 www.maritz.com/~/media/Files/MaritzDotCom/White%20Papers/ExcecutiveSummary_Research.ashx

30 Rob Goffee and Gareth Jones, Why should anyone be led by you? (2015).

31 Stephen MR Covey, The speed of trust (2006).

32 Robert Cialdini, Influence: the psychology of persuasion (2007).

33 Rob Goffee and Gareth Jones, Why should anyone be led by you? (2015).

34 Eric Berne, Games people play (1964).

35 Thomas Harris, I'm OK, you're OK (2012).

36 Roger Fisher and Daniel Shapiro, Beyond reason (2006).

37 Mark Murphy, "All great leadership styles begin with spending more time with employees" at Leadershipiq.com (22 June 2015)

www.leadershipiq.com/blogs/leadershipiq/35352257-all-great-leadership-styles-begin-by-spending-time-with-employees (accessed February 2018).

38 Otto Kroeger, Type talk at work (1989).

39 Gavin Kennedy, Everything is negotiable (2008).

40 Stephen Covey, The 7 habits of highly effective people (2004).

41 Caroline Webb, How to have a good day (2016).

42 Centre for Effective Dispute Resolution, "Tough times, tough talk. A guide to working life conflicts" at Cedr.com (September 2010) www.cedr.com/about_us/toughtalk/ (accessed February 2018).

43 Nancy Kline, Time to think (2002).

44 Daniel Kahneman, Thinking fast and slow (2012).

45 Malcolm Gladwell, Blink: the power of thinking without thinking (2006).

46 Nancy Kline, Time to Think (Cassell, 2002).

47 Ibid, page 91.

48 Stephen Covey, The 7 habits of highly effective people (2004).

49 Susan Cain, Quiet: the power of the introvert in a world that can't stop talking (2013).

50 David A. Garvin, "How Google sold its managers on Management" at HBR.com (December 2013) https://hbr.org/2013/12/how-google-sold-its-engineers-on-management (accessed February 2018).

51 Caroline Webb, How to have a good day (2016).

52 Ibid.

53 Kevan Hall, Speed lead (2007).

54 Nancy Kline, Time to think (2002).

55 Marcus Buckingham, Now discover your strengths (2004).

56 Corporate Leadership Council, "Building the high performance workforce" at squawkpoint.com (2002) www.squawkpoint.

com/wp-content/uploads/2017/02/CLC_Building_the_High_
Performance_Workforce_A_Quantitative_Analysis_of_the_
Effectiveness_of_Performance_Management_Strategies1.pdf
(accessed February 2018).

[57] Caroline Webb, How to have a good day (2016).

[58] Ibid.

[59] David McNally, Even eagles need a push (1993).

[60] Stephen Covey, The 7 habits of highly effective people (2004).

[61] Simon Sinek, Start with why (2011).

[62] Emily Fletcher, Gary A Abel, Rob Anderson, Suzanne H
Richards, Chris Salisbury, Sarah Gerard Dean, Anna Sansom,
Fiona C Warren and John L Campbell, "Quitting patient care
and career break intentions among general practitioners in
South West England: findings of a census survey of general
practitioners" at Bmjopen.bmj.com (10 March 2017) http://
bmjopen.bmj.com/content/bmjopen/7/4/e015853.full.pdf
(accessed February 2018).

[63] Michael Harris, "I have forgotten how to read" at
Theglobeandmail.com (February 2018) www.theglobeandmail.
com/opinion/i-have-forgotten-how-toread/article37921379/#_=_
(accessed March 2018).

[64] Matthew Walker, "The sleep deprivation epidemic" at
thersa.org (23 October 2017) www.thersa.org/discover/
videos/event-videos/2017/10/matthew-walker-on-the-
sleep-deprivation-epidemic?gclid=EAIaIQobChMI486_
r7ql2QIVr7ftCh3sWAsKEAAYASAAEgJq2PD_BwE (accessed
February 2018).

[65] Caroline Webb, How to have a good day (2016).